GUIDE TO EXTERNAL DEGREE PROGRAMS IN THE UNITED STATES

GUIDE TO EXTERNAL DEGREE PROGRAMS IN THE UNITED STATES

Second Edition

Edited by
EUGENE SULLIVAN

American Council on Education • Macmillan Publishing Company
NEW YORK

Collier Macmillan Publishers
LONDON

Copyright © 1983 by American Council on Education and Macmillan
Publishing Company

The American Council on Education/Macmillan Series in Higher Education

Macmillan Publishing Co.,
A Division of Macmillan, Inc.   .
866 Third Avenue, New York, N.Y. 10022

Collier Macmillan Canada, Inc.

Library of Congress Catalog Card Number: 83–7049

Printed in the United States of America

printing number
1   2   3   4   5   6   7   8   9   10

Library of Congress Cataloging in Publication Data

Main entry under title:

Guide to external degree programs in the United
    States.

    (The American Council on Education/Macmillan
series in higher education)
    Includes index.
    1. Degrees, Academic—United States.   2. University
extension—United States.   3. Correspondence schools
and courses—United States.   4. College credits—
United States.   I. Sullivan, Eugene J.   II. American
Council on Education.   III. Series.
LB2381.G84   1983   378'.24'0973   83–7049
ISBN 0-02-932350-9

Contents

Preface

This second edition of the *Guide to External Degree Programs in the United States* includes new undergraduate and graduate programs as well as updated revisions of those published in the first edition. These programs are designed to meet the needs of the working person and other part-time students, who because of time, financial, or other limitations cannot complete a degree program in the traditional way requiring attendance of on-campus classes. Thus, they afford individuals access to higher education that would otherwise not be available to them.

Off-campus instructional methods range from independent study projects and correspondence courses to computer-assisted learning and telecommunications technology. These methods have proven to be as effective as regular classroom teaching and are academically sound. In addition, they provide for a more individualized style of teaching and learning. Instruction is supplemented in most programs by such learner support services as academic and career counseling, financial aid, and job-placement assistance.

Another important characteristic of external degree programs is that they award credit for an individual's prior college-level learning. Many educators have realized that opportunities for learning abound in the workplace and in a variety of other settings outside the education establishment and that sound pedagogy requires the recognition of such learning. In 1978 a joint recommendation of the Council on Postsecondary Accreditation (COPA), the American Council on Education (ACE), and the American Association of Collegiate Registrars and Admissions Officers (AACRAO) encouraged recognition of such credit: "Transfer-of-credit policies should encompass educational accomplishment attained in extrainstitutional settings as well as at accredited postsecondary institutions" (see Appendix A).

Institutions accredited by a COPA-recognized agency are listed in this guide. Many of the external degree programs offered by these institutions are either traditional liberal acts concentrations or individually designed studies that enable the student to structure the program to meet his or her particular interests. Other types offered are occupationally oriented programs (e.g., business administration, nursing, computer science, and so forth) or applied programs in the social sciences (e.g., human services, urban and environmental planning, and so forth).

The format of the listed entries is intended to provide the reader with essential but not exhaustive information on programs offered. Information listed includes the institution's accreditation, acceptance of out-of-state students and tuition differential, minimum campus time, instructional methods provided for off-campus learning and student support services; but information about such matters as maximum credit awarded for prior or experiential learning is not given. The latter kind of information cannot be generalized because such learning will be applied to a student's particular academic program and learning goals. Specific information such as this should be sought from the college or university.

The increased educational opportunities available through external degree programs also point to the importance of individuals assuming greater decision-making responsibility for selecting programs that are particularly suited to their own learning needs. This publication is intended to contribute toward this end.

I wish to thank the institutions that participated in the update of this new edition for their cooperation and warm support. Special thanks are due to Valerie Holland for her painstaking care in typing the entire manuscript.

Eugene Sullivan
Associate Director
Office on Educational Credit and Credentials
American Council on Education

Terminology

External Degree Program — For purposes of this guide, an external degree program is defined as an academic program offered by an accredited institution that stipulates that less than 25 percent of the degree requirements be campus based and that provides instruction for off-campus learning. (Institutions whose missions do not include the provision of instruction but that award credit for various types of prior learning and for passing standardized credit-by-examinations, however, are included as exceptions.)

Most of the institutions included in the guide generally grant credit for documented prior learning (see definition below) and also provide a variety of student support services.

Prior Learning — External degree programs distinguish between two types of prior learning: (a) prior formal classroom or institution-sponsored learning, usually in the form of courses or structured formal instruction offered by businesses, government agencies, labor unions, professional or voluntary associations, and the military; and (2) prior experiential learning acquired on an individual basis through work experience, travel, self-study, and so forth.

In order to receive academic credit, both types of prior learning must be documented and assessable. Documentation may include standardized examinations, transcripts from accredited institutions, official military records, letters of evaluation from employers, portfolios, and so forth. Third-party assessments, such as those provided by the American Council on Education, are frequently required by colleges and universities for programs offered by sponsors other than postsecondary institutions.

The Guide

Institutions offering external degree programs are listed alphabetically by state. For each institution is given the mailing address that was current as of fall 1982 followed by fifteen items describing the program.

1. The **degree title** and the **areas of study** available. Some institutions offer degrees without designating a specific major. They include the following degrees: Associate of Arts or Science, Bachelor of Arts or Science, Associate or Bachelor's of General Studies, Associate or Bachelor's of Liberal Studies, Associate or Bachelor's in Liberal Arts, Associate in Bachelor's in Individual-ized Studies, and the Associate Degree.

2. **Institutional accreditation** by an accrediting commission or association of schools and colleges recognized by the Council on Postsecondary Accredita-tion. These commissions or associations credential total operating units only, not parts of them. Institutions listed in this guide are fully accredited (see *Accredited Institutions of Postsecondary Education, Programs, Candidates,* published for the Council on Postsecondary Accreditation by the American Council on Education in Appendix c).

3. The **kind or amount of previous education** required for admission to the program. The GED, frequently noted, refers to the General Educational Development Testing Program, which provides a means for assessment of high school graduation equivalency. Other qualifications may also be noted.

4. **Academic credit practices regarding prior learning** (see the definition of prior learning under "Terminology").

5. **Academic credit practices regarding standardized achievement tests**, which are administered on a national, regional, state, or interinstitutional basis.

6. The **number of semester or quarter hours** requried to receive a degree, or other requirements if the institution is not on a semester or quarter system.

7. The **minimum on-campus time** required for study in order to complete the program.
8. The **kinds of instruction for off-campus learning** available to the student.
9. **Student support services** provided.
10. **Available informational materials**.
11. The **grading system** used to evaluate the student's work while enrolled in the program.
12. The **enrollment** as of 1982.
13. The **number of external degrees** conferred by the program through 1981.
14. The **year** in which the program began.
15. The institution's policy regarding the acceptance of **out-of-state students** in the program and the tuition differential for these students.

GUIDE TO EXTERNAL DEGREE PROGRAMS IN THE UNITED STATES

PROGRAMS

Samford University

800 Lakeshore Drive
Birmingham, AL 35229

1. **Degrees and areas of study:** Bachelor of General Studies
2. **Institutional accreditation:** Southern Association of Colleges and Schools
3. **Previous education required:** One to two years of college
4. **Credit for prior learning:** Satisfactory completion of instruction offered by businesses, government agencies, labor unions, or professional or voluntary associations, and evaluated by the American Council on Education; credit upon transfer from other institutions; demonstrated experiential learning (life and occupational experiences); military educational experiences evaluated by the American Council on Education
5. **Credit for successful completion of standardized achievement tests:** College-Level Examination Program (CLEP) General Examinations, College-Level Examination Program (CLEP) Subject Examinations, College Board Advanced Placement Examinations, DANTES Subject Standardized Tests (DSST)
6. **Number of credit hours required for degree:** 128 semester hours
7. **Minimum campus time:** None
8. **Instructional methods provided for off-campus learning:** Video cassettes, guided instruction via telephone and mail, packaged course and study guides, cooperative education, supervised field work
9. **Student support services provided:** Academic advising, financial aid, orientation, counseling and testing, career counseling, job placement assistance
10. **Available informational materials:** Student handbook of pertinent policies and procedures, program brochure, program included in master catalog
11. **Grading system:** A, B, C, D, F, or other variation of scale using A, B, C
12. **Enrollment:** 400
13. **Degrees conferred:** 81
14. **Year begun:** 1976
15. **Out-of-state students:** Accepted; tuition higher than for in-state students

University of Alabama

New College
External Degree Program
P. O. Drawer ED
University, AL 35486

1. **Degrees and areas of study:** Bachelor of Arts or Science. The program offers an interdisciplinary degree in seven major areas: human services, social sciences, humanities, natural sciences, applied sciences, administrative sciences, and communication

2. **Institutional accreditation:** Southern Association of Colleges and Schools

3. **Previous education required:** High school diploma or GED equivalent

4. **Credit for prior learning:** Satisfactory completion of instruction offered by businesses, government agencies, labor unions, or professional or voluntary associations, and evaluated by the American Council on Education; credit upon transfer from other institutions: demonstrated experiential learning (life and occupational experiences); military educational experiences evaluated by the American Council on Education

5. **Credit for successful completion of standardized achievement tests:** College-Level Examination Program (CLEP) General Examinations, College-Level Examination Program (CLEP) Subject Examinations, College Board Advanced Placement Examinations, American College Testing (ACT) Proficiency Examination Program, DANTES Subject Standardized Tests (DSST), Certified Professional Secretary Examination, Certified Court Room Reporters Examination

6. **Number of credit hours required for degree:** 128 semester hours

7. **Minimum campus time:** Two-day orientation seminar

8. **Instructional methods provided for off-campus learning:** Correspondence courses, television courses, newspaper courses, guided instruction via telephone and mail, computer-assisted, self-paced instruction, packaged course and study guides, cooperative education, supervised field work, sponsored field work, sponsored experiential learning, contract learning plan between the student and faculty member and/or project director

9. **Student support services provided:** Academic advising, financial aid, orientation, counseling and testing, career counseling, job placement assistance

10. **Available informational materials:** Student handbook of pertinent policies and procedures, program catalog, program brochure, Guide to Prior Learning, Guide to Portfolio Development, Guide to Contract Development, Newsletter

11. **Grading system:** There is no predominant grading system; type of evaluation varies according to agreement between student and advisor/mentor/instructor

12. **Enrollment:** 450

13. **Degrees conferred:** 238

14. **Year begun:** 1973

15. **Out-of-state students:** Accepted; tuition same as for in-state students

Antioch University/West

650 Pine Street
San Francisco, CA 94018

23 West Mission Street
Santa Barbara, CA 93101

931 University Boulevard #309
Honolulu, HI 96829

835 Delaware Street
Denver, CO 80204

1729 17th Avenue
Seattle, WA 98122

300 Rose Avenue
Venice, CA 90291

1. **Degrees and areas of study:** Bachelor of Arts in Liberal Studies
2. **Institutional accreditation:** North Central Association of Colleges and Schools
3. **Previous education required:** High school diploma or GED equivalency
4. **Credit for prior learning:** Credit upon transfer from other institutions; demonstrated experiential learning (life and occupational experiences); military educational experiences evaluated by the American Council on Education
5. **Credit for successful completion of standardized achievement tests:** None
6. **Number of credit hours required for degree:** 180 quarter hours
7. **Minimum campus time:** 36 quarter hours in coursework which may be a combination of university-sponsored courses on campus and off-campus learning in internships, workshops in the community, etc.
8. **Instructional methods provided for off-campus learning:** Guided instruction via telephone and mail, sponsored experiential learning
9. **Student support services provided:** Academic advising, financial aid, orientation
10. **Available informational materials:** Student handbook of pertinent policies and procedures, program brochure
11. **Grading system:** Narrative evaluation by evaluator/instructor and self-assessment by student
12. **Enrollment:** 450
13. **Degrees conferred:** 2,189
14. **Year begun:** 1971
15. **Out-of-state students:** Accepted; tuition same as for in-state students

California College for Respiratory Therapy

Correspondence Division
1810 State Street
San Diego, CA 92101

1. **Degrees and areas of study:** Associate in Applied Science in Respiratory Therapy
2. **Institutional accreditation:** American Medical Association (AMA) Committee on Allied Health Education and Accreditation, National Home Study Council
3. **Previous education required:** High school diploma or GED equivalent plus enrollment in or graduation from an AMA-accredited Respiratory Therapist Program
4. **Credit for prior learning:** Credit upon transfer from other institutions; military educational experiences evaluated by the American Council on Education
5. **Credit for successful completion of standardized achievement tests:** None
6. **Number of credit hours required for degree:** Successful completion of AMA Respiratory Therapist Program and general science requirements plus 12 semester hours in general humanities for a minimum of 60 semester hours
7. **Minimum campus time:** None
8. **Instructional methods provided for off-campus learning:** Correspondence courses, guided instruction via telephone and mail, packaged course and study guides
9. **Student support services provided:** Academic advising, counseling and testing, career counseling
10. **Available informational materials:** Program catalog, application and official program planning sheet
11. **Grading system:** A, B, C, D, F, or other variation of scale using A, B, C
12. **Enrollment:** None
13. **Degrees conferred:** None
14. **Year begun:** 1982
15. **Out-of-state students:** Accepted; tuition same as for in-state students

California State University—Chico

Center for Regional and Continuing Education
Chico, CA 95929

1. **Degrees and areas of study:** Bachelor of Arts in Liberal Studies, Bachelor of Arts in Social Science, Bachelor of Arts in Business Administration, Bachelor of Arts in Computer Science, Bachelor of Arts in Public Administration, Master of Arts in Computer Science, Master of Public Administration
2. **Institutional accreditation:** North Central Association of Colleges and Schools
3. **Previous education required:** Bachelor, one to two years of college; Master, Bachelor's degree

4. **Credit for prior learning:** Credit upon transfer from other institutions; demonstrated experiential learning (life and occupational experiences); military educational experiences evaluated by the American Council on Education

5. **Credit for successful completion of standardized achievement tests:** College-Level Examination Program (CLEP) General Examinations, College-Level Examination Program (CLEP) Subject Examinations

6. **Number of credit hours required for degree:** Bachelor, 124 semester hours; Master of Arts in Computer Science, 30 semester hours; Master of Public Administration, 36 semester hours

7. **Minimum campus time:** None

8. **Instructional methods provided for off-campus learning:** Television courses, guided instruction via telephone and mail, cooperative education, supervised field work

9. **Student support services provided:** Academic advising, financial aid, orientation

10. **Available informational materials:** Student handbook of pertinent policies and procedures, program brochure

11. **Grading system:** A, B, C, D, F, or other variation of scale using A, B, C

12. **Enrollment:** Bachelor of Arts in Liberal Studies, 30; Bachelor of Arts in Social Science, 30; Bachelor of Arts in Business Administration, 30; Bachelor of Arts in Computer Science, 40; Bachelor of Arts in Public Administration, 40; Master of Arts in Computer Science, 15; Master of Arts in Public Administration, 15

13. **Degrees conferred:** Bachelor of Arts in Liberal Studies, 125 (estimate); Bachelor of Arts in Social Science, 125 (estimate); Bachelor of Arts in Business Administration, 75 (estimate); Bachelor of Arts in Computer Science, 10; Bachelor of Arts in Public Administration, 200 (estimate); Master of Arts in Computer Science, 3; Master of Arts in Public Administration, 50 (estimate)

14. **Year begun:** Bachelor of Arts in Public Administration and Master of Arts in Public Administration, 1970; Bachelor of Arts in Social Science and Bachelor of Arts in Business Administration, 1972; Bachelor of Arts in Computer Science and Master of Arts in Computer Science, 1979; Bachelor of Arts in Liberal Studies, 1974

15. **Out-of-state students:** Accepted; tuition same as for in-state students

California State University, The Consortium

400 Golden Shore
Long Beach, CA 90802

1. **Degrees and areas of study:** Bachelor of Science in Nursing, Bachelor of Science in Vocational Education, Bachelor of Science in Health Care Administration, Master of Arts in Vocational Education, Master in Public Administration, Master of Science in Health Care Administration, Master of Art in Environmental Planning

2. **Institutional accreditation:** Western Association of Schools and Colleges

3. **Previous education required:** Bachelor of Science in Nursing, one to two years of college and license as a Registered Nurse (R.N.); Bachelor of Science in Vocational Education and Bachelor of Science in Health Care Administration, one to two years of college; Master of Arts in Vocational Education, Master in Public Administration, Master of Science in Health Care Administration and Master of Art in Environmental Planning, baccalaureate degree from accredited institution; grade point average of 2.5 on last 60 transferable semester units attempted

4. **Credit for prior learning:** Satisfactory completion of instruction offered by business, government agencies, labor unions, or professional or voluntary associations and evaluated by the American Council on Education; credit upon transfer from other institutions; demonstrated experiential learning (life and occupational experiences); military educational experiences evaluated by the American Council on Education

5. **Credit for successful completion of standardized achievement tests:** College-Level Examination Program (CLEP) General Examinations, College-Level Examination Program (CLEP) Subject Examinations, College Board Advanced Placement Examinations, American College Testing (ACT) Proficiency Examination Program, DANTES Subject Standardized Tests (DSST)

6. **Number of credit hours required for degree:** Bachelor of Science in Nursing, 132 semester hours; Bachelor of Science in Vocational Education, 128 semester hours; Bachelor of Science in Health Care Administration, 124 semester hours; all Master's degrees, 30 semester hours

7. **Minimum campus time:** None

8. **Instructional methods provided for off-campus learning:** Bachelor of Science in Vocational Education and Bachelor of Science in Health Care Administration, supervised field work, sponsored experiential learning; Master of Arts in Vocational Education, Master in Public Administration, Master of Science in Health Care Administration, Master of Art in Environmental Planning, supervised field work; Bachelor of Science in Nursing, video cassettes, television courses, computer-assisted, self-paced instruction, packaged course and study guides, sponsored experiential learning

9. **Student support services provided:** Bachelor of Science in Nursing, academic advising, financial aid, orientation, counseling and testing, job placement assistance, career counseling; Bachelor of Science in Vocational Education, Bachelor of Science in Health Care Administration, Master of Arts in Vocational Education, Master of Public Administration, Master of Science in Health Care Administration, Master of Art in Environmental Planning, academic advising, financial aid, orientation, counseling and testing, job placement assistance

10. **Available informational materials:** Program catalog, program brochure

11. **Grading system:** A, B, C, D, F, or other variation of scale using A, B, C

12. **Enrollment:** Bachelor of Science in Nursing, 500; Bachelor of Science in Vocational Education, 100; Bachelor of Science in Health Care Administration, 100; Master of Arts in Vocational Education, 200; Master in Public Administration, 300; Master of Science in Health Care Administration, 100; Master of Art in Environmental Planning, 100

13. **Degrees conferred:** Bachelor of Science in Nursing, cannot be estimated; Bachelor of Science in Vocational Education, 50 (estimated); Bachelor of Science in Health Care Administration, 200 (estimated); Master of Arts in Vocational Education, 200 (estimated); Master in Public Administration, 250 (estimated); Master of Science in Health Care Administration, 10 (estimated); Master of Art in Environmental Planning, 50 (estimated)

14. **Year begun:** Bachelor of Science in Vocational Education, 1981; Bachelor of Science in Vocational Education, 1978; Bachelor of Science in Health Care Administration, 1975; Master of Arts in Vocational Education and Master of Art in Environmental Planning, 1975; Master in Public Administration, 1974; Master of Science in Health Care Administration, 1979

15. **Out-of-state students:** Students must reside in state

California State University—Dominquez Hills

1000 East Victoria Street
Carson, CA 90747

1. **Degrees and areas of study:** Bachelor of Arts in the Humanities, Master of Arts in the Humanities, Master of Science in Technology

2. **Institutional accreditation:** Western Association of Schools and Colleges

3. **Previous education required:** Bachelor of Arts in the Humanities, Associate of Arts degree or equivalent; Master of Arts in the Humanities, Bachelor of Art or Science; Master of Science in Technology, Bachelor's degree and California State Licensed Technologist/National Certification

4. **Credit for prior learning:** Bachelor of Arts in the Humanities and Master of Science in Technology, credit upon transfer from other institutions; demonstrated experiential learning (life and occupational experiences); military educational experiences evaluated by the American Council on Education; Master of Arts in the Humanities, credit upon transfer from other institutions; military educational experiences evaluated by the American Council on Education

5. **Credit for successful completion of standardized achievement tests:** Master of Science in Technology, College-Level Examination Program (CLEP) Subject Examinations

6. **Number of credit hours required for degree:** Bachelor of Arts in the Humanities, 186 quarter hours; Master of Arts in the Humanities and Master of Science in Technology, 45 quarter hours

7. **Minimum campus time:** None

8. **Instructional methods provided for off-campus learning:** Bachelor of Arts in the Humanities and Master of Arts in the Humanities, correspondence courses, video cassettes, guided instruction via telephone and mail, packaged course and study guides, supervised field work; Master of Science in Technology, video cassettes, computer-assisted, self-paced instruction, packaged course and study guides, supervised field work, sponsored experiential learning

9. **Student support services provided:** Bachelor of Arts in the Humanities and Master of Arts in the Humanities, academic advising; Master of Science in

Technology, academic advising, financial aid, orientation, counseling and testing, job placement assistance

10. **Available informational materials:** Bachelor of Arts in the Humanities and Master of Arts in the Humanities, program catalog, program brochure; Master of Science in Technology, student handbook of pertinent policies and procedures, program catalog, program brochure

11. **Grading system:** A, B, C, D, F, or other variation of scale using A, B, C

12. **Enrollment:** Bachelor of Arts in the Humanities and Master of Arts in the Humanities, 175; Master of Science in Technology, 250

13. **Degrees conferred:** Bachelor of Arts in the Humanities, 33 (estimated); Master of Arts in the Humanities, 144 (estimated); Master of Science in Technology, 500 (estimated)

14. **Year begun:** 1974

15. **Out-of-state students:** Accepted; tuition same as for in-state students

Coastline Community College

11460 Warner Avenue
Fountain Valley, CA 92708

1. **Degrees and areas of study:** Associate in Arts

2. **Institutional accreditation:** Western Association of Schools and Colleges

3. **Previous education required:** High school or 18 years of age

4. **Credit for prior learning:** Satisfactory completion of instruction offered by businesses, government agencies, labor unions, or professional or voluntary associations, and evaluated by the American Council on Education; credit upon transfer from other institutions; demonstrated experiential learning (life and occupational experiences); military educational experiences evaluated by the American Council on Education

5. **Credit for successful completion of standardized achievement tests:** College-Level Examination Program (CLEP) General Examinations, College-Level Examination Program (CLEP) Subject Examinations, American College Testing (ACT) Proficiency Examination Program, College Board Advanced Placement Examinations, DANTES Subject Standardized Tests (DSST)

6. **Number of credit hours required for degree:** 60 semester hours

7. **Minimum campus time:** None

8. **Instructional methods provided for off-campus learning:** Video cassettes, television courses, newspaper courses, guided instruction via telephone and mail, packaged course and study guides, cooperative education

9. **Student support services provided:** Academic advising, financial aid, orientation, counseling and testing, career counseling

10. **Available informational materials:** Student handbook of pertinent policies and procedures, individual brochures and information contained in class schedule

11. **Grading system:** Pass/fail, credit/no credit, or other variation of this scale
12. **Enrollment:** 50 to 100
13. **Degrees conferred:** 100 (estimated)
14. **Year begun:** 1976
15. **Out-of-state students:** Accepted; tuition higher than for in-state students

Fielding Institute

226 E. de la Guerra Street
Santa Barbara, CA 93101

1. **Degrees and areas of study:** The Fielding Institute is an external degree graduate school for mid-career studies offering degrees in professional psychology and in human and organization development. The degrees are: Master of Arts, Doctor of Philosophy, Doctor of Psychology, Doctor of Education, and Doctor of Human Services
2. **Institutional accreditation:** Western Association of Schools and Colleges
3. **Previous education required:** Master's degree for the doctoral program, baccalaureate degree plus work experience for the master's program
4. **Credit for prior learning:** None
5. **Credit for successful completion of standardized achievement tests:** None
6. **Number of credit hours required for degree:** Competency based on knowledge areas; training areas, internship, and dissertation
7. **Minimum campus time:** An Admissions Contract Workshop of five days in Santa Barbara, California; a contract review each year, of no less than one day per year; and three final reviews: A Comprehensive Assessment, a Professional Assessment, and a Final Review of the Dissertation
8. **Instructional methods provided for off-campus learning:** Correspondence courses, video cassettes, television courses, guided instruction via telephone and mail, computer-assisted, self-paced instruction, packaged course and study guides, cooperative education, supervised field work, sponsored experiential learning
9. **Student support services provided:** Academic advising, financial aid, orientation, counseling and testing, career counseling, job placement assistance
10. **Available informational materials:** Student handbook of pertinent policies and procedures, program catalog, program brochure
11. **Grading system:** A, B, C, D, F, or other variation of scale using A, B, C, and pass/fail, credit/no credit, or other variation of this scale
12. **Enrollment:** 450
13. **Degrees conferred:** 150
14. **Year begun:** 1974
15. **Out-of-state students:** Accepted; tuition same as for in-state students

University of LaVerne

School of Continuing Education
1950 Third Street
LaVerne, CA 91750

1. **Degrees and areas of study:** Bachelor of Science in Health Care Management, Master of Science in Health Care Management

2. **Institutional accreditation:** Western Association of Schools and Colleges

3. **Previous education required:** Bachelor of Science in Health Care Management, high school diploma or GED equivalent; Master of Science in Health Care Management, baccalaureate degree

4. **Credit for prior learning:** Satisfactory completion of instruction offered by businesses, government agencies, labor unions, or professional or voluntary associations, and evaluated by the American Council on Education; credit upon transfer from other institutions; demonstrated experiential learning (life and occupational experiences); military educational experiences evaluated by the American Council on Education

5. **Credit for successful completion of standardized achievement tests:** College-Level Examination Program (CLEP) General Examinations, College-Level Examination Program (CLEP) Subject Examinations, College Board Advanced Placement Examinations, American College Testing (ACT) Proficiency Examination Program

6. **Number of credit hours required for degree:** Bachelor of Science in Health Care Management, 128 semester hours; Master of Science in Health Care Management, 33 semester hours

7. **Minimum campus time:** None

8. **Instructional methods provided for off-campus learning:** Supervised field work, sponsored experiential learning

9. **Student support services provided:** Academic advising, financial aid, orientation, counseling and testing, job placement assistance

10. **Available informational materials:** Student handbook of pertinent policies and procedures, program catalog, program brochure; university background information; faculty vitaes

11. **Grading system:** A, B, C, D, F, or other variation of scale using A, B, C

12. **Enrollment:** Bachelor of Science in Health Care Management, 135; Master of Science Health Care Management, 135

13. **Degrees conferred:** Bachelor of Science in Health Care Management, 20; Master of Science in Health Care Management, 33

14. **Year begun:** 1978

15. **Out-of-state students:** Accepted; tuition same as for in-state students

Loretto Heights College

University Without Walls
3001 South Federal Blvd.
Denver, CO 80236

1. **Degrees and areas of study:** Bachelor of Arts (selected majors); Bachelor of Arts in Competency-Based Teacher Education
2. **Institutional accreditation:** North Central Association of Colleges and Schools
3. **Previous education required:** High school diploma or GED equivalent
4. **Credit for prior learning:** Satisfactory completion of instruction offered by businesses, government agencies, labor unions, or professional or voluntary associations, and evaluated by the American Council on Education; credit upon transfer from other institutions; demonstrated experiential learning (life and occupational experiences); military educational experiences evaluated by the American Council on Education
5. **Credit for successful completion of standardized achievement tests:** College-Level Examination Program (CLEP) General Examinations, College-Level Examination Program (CLEP) Subject Examination Program, College Board Advanced Placement Examinations, DANTES Subject Standardized Tests (DSST)
6. **Number of credit hours required for degree:** 128 semester hours
7. **Minimum campus time:** Bachelor of Arts, one all-day orientation and periodic meetings depending on individual program; Bachelor of Arts in Competency-Based Teacher Education, one-day orientation and a weekly three-hour seminar
8. **Instructional methods provided for off-campus learning:** Bachelor of Arts, television courses, newspaper courses, computer-assisted, self-paced instruction, packaged course and study guides, cooperative education, supervised field work, sponsored experiential learning; Bachelor of Arts in Competency-Based Teacher Education, correspondence courses, video cassettes, television courses, newspaper courses, guided instruction via telephone and mail, computer-assisted, self-paced instruction, packaged course and study guides, cooperative education, supervised field work, sponsored experiential learning
9. **Student support services provided:** Academic advising, financial aid, orientation, counseling and testing, career counseling, job placement assistance
10. **Available informational materials:** Student handbook of pertinent policies and procedures, program brochure, Colorado Department of Education requirements for certification
11. **Grading system:** A, B, C, D, F, or other variation of scale using A, B, C, and pass/fail, credit/no credit, or other variation of this scale

12. **Enrollment:** Bachelor of Arts, 82; Bachelor of Arts in Competency-Based Teacher Education, 13

13. **Degrees conferred:** Bachelor of Arts, 470; Bachelor of Arts in Competency-Based Teacher Education, cannot be estimated

14. **Year begun:** Bachelor of Arts, 1971; Bachelor of Arts in Competency-Based Teacher Education, 1974

15. **Out-of-state students:** Bachelor of Arts, accepted, tuition same as for in-state students; Bachelor of Arts in Competency-Based Teacher Education, not accepted

CONNECTICUT

Trinity College

Individualized Degree Program
Hartford, CT 06106

1. **Degrees and areas of study:** Bachelor of Arts, Bachelor of Science (individually designed studies)
2. **Institutional accreditation:** New England Association of Schools and Colleges
3. **Previous education required:** High school diploma or GED equivalent
4. **Credit for prior learning:** Credit upon transfer from other institutions
5. **Credit for successful completion of standardized achievement tests:** College Board Advanced Placement Examinations, International Baccalaureate Higher Level Examinations
6. **Number of credit hours for degree:** 36 course credits (one course credit = 3 semester hours)
7. **Minimum campus time:** One day per month
8. **Instructional methods provided for off-campus learning:** Packaged course and study guides, sponsored experiential learning
9. **Student support services provided:** Academic advising, financial aid, orientation, counseling and testing, career counseling
10. **Available informatinal materials:** Student handbook of pertinent policies and procedures, program catalog, program brochure
11. **Grading system:** A, B, C, D, F, or other variation of scale using A, B, C
12. **Enrollment:** 98
13. **Degrees conferred:** 53
14. **Year begun:** 1973
15. **Out-of-state students:** Accepted; tuition same as for in-state students

FLORIDA

Eckerd College

Program for Experienced Learners
P. O. Box 124560
St. Petersburg, FL 33733

1. **Degrees and areas of study:** Bachelor of Arts, Bachelor of Science
2. **Institutional accreditation:** Southern Association of Colleges and Schools
3. **Previous education required:** High school diploma or GED equivalency
4. **Credit for prior learning:** Satisfactory completion of instruction offered by businesses, government agencies, labor unions, or professional or voluntary associations, and evaluated by the American Council on Education; credit upon transfer from other institutions; demonstrated experiential learning (life and occupational experiences); military educational experiences evaluated by the American Council on Education
5. **Credit for successful completion of standardized achievement tests:** College-Level Examination Program (CLEP) General Examinations, College-Level Examination Program (CLEP) Subject Examinations, College Board Advanced Placement Examinations, American College Testing (ACT) Proficiency Examination Program, DANTES Subject Standardized Tests (DSST)
6. **Number of credit hours required for degree:** 36 courses
7. **Minimum campus time:** None
8. **Instructional methods provided for off-campus learning:** Correspondence courses, guided instruction via telephone and mail, packaged course and study guides, cooperative education, supervised field work, sponsored experiential learning
9. **Student support services provided:** Academic advising, counseling and testing, career counseling
10. **Available informational materials:** Program catalog, program brochure
11. **Grading system:** A, B, C, D, F, or other variation of scale using A, B, C
12. **Enrollment:** 700
13. **Degrees conferred:** 112
14. **Year begun:** 1978
15. **Out-of-state students:** Accepted; tuition same as for in-state students

University of South Florida

Division of Special Degree Programs
School of Continuing Education
4202 Fowler Avenue
Tampa, FL 33620

1. **Degrees and areas of study:** Bachelor of Independent Studies

2. **Institutional accreditation:** Southern Association of Colleges and Schools

3. **Previous education required:** High school diploma or GED equivalency

4 & 5. **Credit for prior learning and successful completion of standardized tests:** No recognition or award of credit hours per se; prior learning is recognized via (1) an accelerated reading program, or (2) challenge tutorial by exam or interface with selected associate credentials

6. **Number of credit hours required for degree:** The program does not operate under a credit-hour system. The student must fulfill requirements in the humanities, natural sciences, and social sciences, and complete a thesis to receive the degree

7. **Minimum campus time:** Four to six weeks of seminar experience

8. **Instructional methods provided for off-campus learning:** Tutorials, thesis experience

9. **Student support services provided:** Academic advising, financial aid, orientation, counseling and testing

10. **Available informational materials:** Program brochure, *Student Guide to Independent Study*, Profile of Program and Population, newsletter

11. **Grading system:** Satisfactory (S); pass with deficiency (PWD); unsatisfactory (U)

12. **Enrollment:** 115

13. **Degrees conferred:** 55

14. **Year begun:** 1968

15. **Out-of-state students:** Accepted; tuition same as for in-state students

Black Hawk College

6600 34th Avenue
Moline, IL 61265

1. **Degrees and areas of study:** Associate of Arts in Liberal Studies
2. **Institutional accreditation:** North Central Association of Colleges and Schools
3. **Previous education required:** High school diploma or GED equivalent
4. **Credit for prior learning:** Satisfactory completion of instruction offered by businesses, government agencies, labor unions, or professional or voluntary associations, and evaluated by the American Council on Education; credit upon transfer from other institutions; demonstrated experiential learning (life and occupational experiences); military educational experiences evaluated by the American Council on Education
5. **Credit for successful completion of standardized achievement tests:** College-Level Examination Program (CLEP) General Examinations, College-Level Examination Program (CLEP) Subject Examinations, American College Testing (ACT) Proficiency Examination Program, College Board Advanced Placement Examinations
6. **Number of credit hours required for degree:** 62 semester hours
7. **Minimum campus time:** None
8. **Instructional methods provided for off-campus learning:** Video cassettes, television courses, newspaper courses, packaged course and study guides
9. **Student support services provided:** Academic advising, financial aid, orientation, counseling and testing, career counseling, job placement assistance
10. **Available informational materials:** Student handbook of pertinent policies and procedures
11. **Grading system:** A, B, C, D, F, or other variation of scale using A, B, C
12. **Enrollment:** 50
13. **Degrees conferred:** 90 (estimated)
14. **Year begun:** 1976
15. **Out-of-state students:** Not accepted

Chicago State University

95th Street at King Drive
Chicago, IL 60628
Member of the Board of Governors Bachelor of Arts Degree Program

1. **Degrees and areas of study:** Bachelor of Arts
2. **Institutional accreditation:** North Central Association of Colleges and Schools
3. **Previous education required:** High school diploma or GED equivalency
4. **Credit for prior learning:** Satisfactory completion of instruction offered by businesses, government agencies, labor unions, or professional or voluntary associations, and evaluated by the American Council on Education; credit upon transfer from other institutions; demonstrated experiential learning (life and occupational experiences); military educational experiences evaluated by the American Council on Education
5. **Credit for successful completion of standardized achievement tests:** College-Level Examination Program (CLEP) General Examinations, College-Level Examination Program (CLEP) Subject Examinations, American College Testing (ACT) Proficiency Examination Program, College Board Advanced Placement Examinations, DANTES Subject Standardized Tests (DSST)
6. **Number of credit hours for degree:** 120 semester hours
7. **Minimum campus time:** None
8. **Instructional methods provided for off-campus learning:** Correspondence courses, newspaper courses, guided instruction via telephone and mail, packaged course and study guides, sponsored experiential learning
9. **Student support services provided:** Academic advising, financial aid, orientation, counseling and testing, job placement assistance, career counseling
10. **Available informational materials:** Student handbook of pertinent policies and procedures, program brochure
11. **Grading system:** A, B, C, D, F, or other variation of scale using A, B, C
12. **Enrollment:** 1200
13. **Degrees conferred:** 693
14. **Year begun:** 1973
15. **Out-of-state students:** Accepted; tuition higher than for in-state students

College of DuPage

22nd and Lambert
Glen Ellyn, IL 60137

1. **Degrees and areas of study:** Associate of Arts in Liberal Arts
2. **Institutional accreditation:** North Central Association of Colleges and Schools
3. **Previous education required:** High school diploma or GED equivalent
4. **Credit for prior learning:** Credit upon transfer from other institutions; demonstrated experiential learning (life and occupational experiences); military educational experiences evaluated by the American Council on Education
5. **Credit for successful completion of standardized achievement tests:** College-Level Examination Program (CLEP) General Examinations, College-Level

Examination Program (CLEP) Subject Examinations, College Board Advanced Placement Examinations

6. **Number of credit hours for degree:** 93 quarter hours
7. **Minimum campus time:** None
8. **Instructional methods provided for off-campus learning:** Video cassettes, television courses, newspaper courses, computer-assisted, self-paced instruction, packaged course and study guides, cooperative education, supervised field work, sponsored experiential learning
9. **Student support services provided:** Academic advising, financial aid, counseling and testing, career counseling, job placement assistance
10. **Available informational materials:** Quarterly schedule that describes program opportunities
11. **Grading system:** A, B, C, D, F, or other variation of scale using A, B, C
12. **Enrollment:** 4,000
13. **Degrees conferred:** 5,000 (estimated)
14. **Year begun:** 1972
15. **Out-of-state students:** Accepted; tuition higher than for in-state students

Eastern Illinois University

Charleston, IL 61920
Member of the Board of Governors Bachelor of Arts Degree Program

1. **Degrees and areas of study:** Bachelor of Arts
2. **Institutional accreditation:** North Central Association of Colleges and Schools
3. **Previous education required:** High school diploma or GED equivalent
4. **Credit for prior learning:** Satisfactory completion of instruction offered by businesses, government agencies, labor unions, or professional or voluntary associations, and evaluated by the American Council on Education; credit upon transfer from other institutions; demonstrated experiential learning (life and occupational experiences); military educational experiences evaluated by the American Council on Education
5. **Credit for successful completion of standardized achievement tests:** College-Level Examination Program (CLEP) General Examinations, College-Level Examination Program (CLEP) Subject Examinations, DANTES Subject Standardized Tests (DSST)
6. **Number of credit hours required for degree:** 120 semester hours
7. **Minimum campus time:** None
8. **Instructional methods provided for off-campus learning:** Correspondence courses, video cassettes, television courses, newspaper courses, guided instruction via telephone and mail, computer-assisted, self-paced instruction, packaged course and study guides, cooperative education, supervised field work, sponsored experiential learning

9. **Student support services provided:** Academic advising, financial aid, orientation, counseling and testing, career counseling, job placement assistance

10. **Available informational materials:** Student handbook of pertinent policies and procedures, program catalog, program brochure

11. **Grading system:** A, B, C, D, F, or other variation of scale using A, B, C

12. **Enrollment:** 750

13. **Degrees conferred:** 1,000

14. **Year begun:** 1973

15. **Out-of-state students:** Accepted; tuition higher than for in-state students

Governors State University

Park Forest South, IL 60466
Member of the Board of Governors Bachelor of Arts Degree Program

1. **Degrees and areas of study:** Bachelor of Arts

2. **Institutional accreditation:** North Central Association of Colleges and Schools

3. **Previous education required:** Two years of college; less than high school dipolma by special permission

4. **Credit for prior learning:** Satisfactory completion of instruction offered by businesses, government agencies, labor unions, or professional or voluntary associations, and evaluated by the American Council on Education; credit upon transfer from other institutions; demonstrated experiential learning (life and occupational experiences), military educational experiences evaluated by the American Council on Education

5. **Credit for successful completion of standardized achievement tests:** College-Level Examination Program (CLEP) General Examinations, College-Level Examination Program (CLEP) Subject Examinations, American College Testing (ACT) Proficiency Examination Program, College Board Advanced Placement Examinations, DANTES Subject Standardized Tests (DSST)

6. **Number of credit hours required for degree:** 120 semester hours

7. **Minimum campus time:** None

8. **Instructional methods provided for off-campus learning:** Correspondence courses, television courses, packaged course and study guides, cooperative education, supervised field work, sponsored experiential learning

9. **Student support services provided:** Academic advising, financial aid, orientation, career counseling, job placement assistance

10. **Available informational materials:** Student handbook of pertinent policies and procedures, program brochure, portfolio development materials

11. **Grading system:** A, B, C, D, F, or other variation of scale using A, B, C

12. **Enrollment:** 1,317

13. **Degrees conferred:** 900

14. **Year begun:** 1973

15. **Out-of-state students:** Accepted; tuition higher than for in-state students

Morraine Valley Community College

10900 S, 88th Avenue
Palos Hills, IL 60465

1. **Degrees and areas of study:** Associate of Arts, Associate of Science
2. **Institutional accreditation:** North Central Association of Colleges and Schools
3. **Previous education required:** High school diploma or GED equivalent
4. **Credit for prior learning:** Satisfactory completion of instruction offered by businesses, government agencies, labor unions, or professional or voluntary associations, and evaluated by the American Council on Education; credit upon transfer from other institutions; demonstrated experiential learning (life and occupational experiences); military educational experiences evaluated by the American Council on Education
5. **Credit for successful completion of standardized achievement tests:** College-Level Examination Program (CLEP) General Examinations, College-Level Examination Program (CLEP) Subject Examinations, American College Testing (ACT) Proficiency Examination Program, College Board Advanced Placement Examinations, DANTES Subject Standardized Tests (DSST)
6. **Number of credit hours required for degree:** 62 semester hours
7. **Minimum campus time:** None
8. **Instructional methods provided for off-campus learning:** Correspondence courses, video cassettes, television courses, newspaper courses, computer-assisted, self-paced instruction, packaged course and study guides, sponsored experiential learning
9. **Student support services provided:** Academic advising, financial aid, orientation, counseling and testing, career counseling, job placement assistance
10. **Available informational materials:** Student handbook of pertinent policies and procedures, program catalog, program brochure
11. **Grading system:** A, B, C, D, F, or other variation of scale using A, B, C, and pass/fail, credit/no credit or other variation of this scale
12. **Enrollment:** 1,850
13. **Degrees conferred:** Cannot be estimated
14. **Year begun:** 1974
15. **Out-of-state students:** Accepted; tuition higher than for in-state students

Northeastern Illinois University

University Without Walls Program
5500 North Saint Louis Avenue
Chicago, IL 60625

1. **Degrees and areas of study:** Bachelor of Arts, Bachelor of Science (competency-based programs)

2. **Institutional accreditation:** North Central Association of Colleges and Schools

3. **Previous education required:** High school diploma or GED equivalency

4. **Credit for prior learning:** Satisfactory completion of instruction offered by businesses, government agencies, labor unions, or professional or voluntary associations, and evaluated by the American Council on Education; credit upon transfer from other institutions; demonstrated experiential learning (life and occupational experiences); military educational experiences evaluated by the American Council on Education

5. **Credit for successful completion of standardized achievement tests:** College-Level Examination Program (CLEP) General Examinations, College-Level Examination Program (CLEP) Subject Examinations

6. **Number of credit hours required for degree:** Not applicable; degree is based on successful completion of competency-based programmatic requirements

7. **Minimum campus time:** None

8. **Instructional methods provided for off-campus learning:** Guided instruction via telephone and mail, supervised field work, sponsored experiential learning

9. **Student support services provided:** Academic advising, orientation

10. **Available informational materials:** Student handbook of pertinent policies and procedures, program brochure

11. **Grading system:** There is no predominant grading system; type of evaluation varies according to agreement between student and advisor/mentor/instructor

12. **Enrollment:** 100

13. **Degrees conferred:** 500

14. **Year begun:** 1971

15. **Out-of-state students:** Accepted; tuition higher than for in-state students

Northeastern Illinois University

5500 N. St. Louis Avenue
Chicago, IL 60625
Member of the Board of Govenors Bachelor of Arts Degree Program

1. **Degrees and areas of study:** Bachelor of Arts

2. **Institutional accreditation:** North Central Association of Colleges and Schools

3. **Previous education required:** High school diploma or GED equivalency

4. **Credit for prior learning:** Satisfactory completion of instruction offered by businesses, government agencies, labor unions, or professional or voluntary associations, and evaluated by the American Council on Education; credit upon transfer from other institutions; demonstrated experiential learning (life and occupational experiences); military educational experiences evaluated by the American Council on Education

5. **Credit for successful completion of standardized achievement tests:** College-Level Examination Program (CLEP) General Examinations, College-Level Examination Program (CLEP) Subject Examinations, American College Testing

(ACT) Proficiency Examination Program, DANTES Subject Standardized Tests (DSST)

6. **Number of credit hours required for degree:** 120 semester hours

7. **Minimum campus time:** None

8. **Instructional methods provided for off-campus learning:** Correspondence courses

9. **Student support services provided:** Academic advising, orientation, counseling and testing, job placement assistance

10. **Available informational materials:** Student handbook of pertinent policies and procedures, program brochure

11. **Grading system:** A, B, C, D, F, or other variation of scale using A, B, C

12. **Enrollment:** 2,200

13. **Degrees conferred:** 1,100

14. **Year begun:** 1973

15. **Out-of-state:** Not accepted

Western Illinois University

900 West Adams
Macomb, IL 614
Member of the Board of Govenors Bachelor of Arts Degree Program

1. **Degrees and areas of study:** Bachelor of Arts

2. **Institutional accreditation:** North Central Association of Colleges and Schools

3. **Previous education required:** High school diploma or GED equivalency; less than high school diploma or GED equivalent by special permission

4. **Credit for prior learning:** Satisfactory completion of instruction offered by businesses, government agencies, labor unions, or professional or voluntary associations, and evaluated by the American Council on Education; credit upon transfer from other institutions; demonstrated experiential learning (life and occupational experiences); military educational experiences evaluated by the American Council on Education

5. **Credit for successful completion of standardized achievement tests:** College-Level Examination Program (CLEP) General Examinations, College-Level Examination Program (CLEP) Subject Examinations, American College Testing (ACT) Proficiency Examination Program, College Board Advanced Placement Examinations, DANTES Subject Standardized Tests (DSST)

6. **Number of credit hours required for degree:** 120 semester hours

7. **Minimum campus time:** None

8. **Instructional methods provided for off-campus learning:** Correspondence courses, television courses, newspaper courses, packaged course and study guides, sponsored experiential learning

9. **Student support services provided:** Academic advising, financial aid, orientation, counseling and testing, job placement assistance, career counseling

10. **Available informational materials:** Student handbook of pertinent policies and procedures, program brochure
11. **Grading system:** A, B, C, D, F, or other variation of scale using A, B, C
12. **Enrollment:** 1,913
13. **Degrees conferred:** 582
14. **Year begun:** 1973
15. **Out-of-state students:** Accepted; tuition same as for in-state students

Indiana Institute of Technology

1600 E. Washington Boulevard
Fort Wayne, IN 46803

1. **Degrees and areas of study:** Associate of Science in Business Administration, Bachelor of Science in Business Administration
2. **Institutional accreditation:** North Central Association of Colleges and Schools
3. **Previous education required:** High school diploma or GED equivalent
4. **Credit for prior learning:** Satisfactory completion of instruction offered by businesses, government agencies, labor unions, or professional or voluntary associations, and evaluated by the American Council on Education; credit upon transfer from other institutions; demonstrated experiential learning (life and occupational experiences); military educational experiences evaluated by the American Council on Education
5. **Credit for successful completion of standardized achievement tests:** College-Level Examination Program (CLEP) General Examinations, College-Level Examination Program (CLEP) Subject Examinations, College Board Advanced Placement Examinations, DANTES Subject Standardized Tests (DSST)
6. **Number of credit hours required for degree:** Associate of Science in Business Administration, 60 semester hours; Bachelor of Science in Business Administration, 120 semester hours
7. **Minimum campus time:** None
8. **Instructional methods provided for off-campus learning:** Correspondence courses, guided instruction via telephone and mail, packaged course and study guides
9. **Student support services provided:** Academic advising, financial aid, orientation, counseling and testing, career counseling, job placement assistance
10. **Available informational materials:** Student handbook of pertinent policies and procedures, program catalog, program brochure
11. **Grading system:** A, B, C, D, F, or other variation of scale using A, B, C
12. **Enrollment:** None
13. **Degrees conferred:** None
14. **Year begun:** 1982
15. **Out-of-state students:** Accepted; tuition same as for in-state students

Indiana University at Bloomington

External Degree Program
Division of Continuing Studies
Owen Hall 202
Bloomington, IN 47405

1. **Degrees and areas of study:** Associate of General Studies, Bachelor of General Studies

2. **Institutional accreditation:** North Central Association of Colleges and Schools

3. **Previous education required:** High school diploma or GED equivalency (provisional admission may be granted to students who do not have a high school diploma or GED certificate)

4. **Credit for prior learning:** Satisfactory completion of instruction offered by businesses, government agencies, labor unions, or professional or voluntary associations, and evaluated by the American Council on Education; credit upon transfer from other institutions; demonstrated experiential learning (life and occupational experiences); military educational experiences evaluated by the American Council on Education

5. **Credit for successful completion of standardized achievement tests:** College-Level Examination Program (CLEP) General Examinations, (Humanities only), College-Level Examination Program (CLEP) Subject Examinations, College Board Advanced Placement Examinations, DANTES Subject Standardized Tests (DSST)

6. **Number of credit hours required for degree:** Associate, 60 semeste hours; Bachelor, 120 semester hours

7. **Minimum campus time:** None

8. **Instructional methods provided for off-campus learning:** Correspondence courses, television courses, newspaper courses, packaged course and study guides, cooperative education, supervised field work, sponsored experiential learning

9. **Student support services provided:** Academic advising, financial aid, orientation, counseling and testing, job placement assistance, career counseling

10. **Available informational materials:** Student handbook of pertinent policies and procedures, program brochure, independent study by correspondence catalog, self-acquired competency regulations, and evening class program

11. **Grading system:** A, B, C, D, F, or other variation of scale using A, B, C

12. **Enrollment:** 440

13. **Degrees conferred:** 103

14. **Year begun:** 1976

15. **Out-of-state students:** Accepted; tuition higher than for in-state students except for correspondence courses

Indiana University at Kokomo

External Degree Program
Division of Continuing Education
2300 South Washington Street
Kokomo, IN 46902

1. **Degrees and areas of study:** Associate of General Studies, Bachelor of General Studies

2. **Institutional accreditation:** North Central Association of Colleges and Schools

3. **Previous education required:** High school diploma or GED equivalency or in the absence of either students who complete 12 semester hours successfully may be admitted to the program

4. **Credit for prior learning:** Satisfactory completion of instruction offered by businesses, government agencies, labor unions, or professional or voluntary associations, and evaluated by the American Council on Education; credit upon transfer from other institutions; demonstrated experiential learning (life and occupational experiences); military educational experiences evaluated by the American Council on Education

5. **Credit for successful completion of standardized achievement tests:** College-Level Examination Program (CLEP) General Examinations, College-Level Examination Program (CLEP) Subject Examinations, American College Testing (ACT) Proficiency Examination Program, College Board Advanced Placement Examinations, DANTES Subject Standardized Tests (DSST)

6. **Number of credit hours required for degree:** Associate, 60 semester hours; Bachelor, 120 semester hours

7. **Minimum campus time:** None

8. **Instructional methods provided for off-campus learning:** Correspondence courses, television courses, newspaper courses, packaged course and study guides, cooperative education, supervised field work, sponsored experiential learning

9. **Student support services provided:** Academic advising, financial aid, orientation, counseling and testing, job placement assistance, career counseling

10. **Available informational materials:** Program catalog, program brochure

11. **Grading system:** Predominantly, A, B, C, D, F, or other variation of scale using A, B, C

12. **Enrollment:** 100

13. **Degrees conferred:** Associate, 30; Bachelor, 55

14. **Year begun:** 1975

15. **Out-of-state students:** Accepted; tuition higher than for in-state students except for correspondence courses

Indiana University at South Bend

General Studies Programs
External Degree Program
1700 Mishawaka Avenue
South Bend, IN 46634

1. **Degrees and areas of study:** Associate of General Studies, Bachelor of General Studies

2. **Institutional accreditation:** North Central Association of Colleges and Schools

3. **Previous education required:** High school diploma or GED equivalency for persons under 21; for persons over 21, there is no minimum educational level

4. **Credit for prior learning:** Satisfactory completion of instruction offered by businesses, government agencies, labor unions, or professional or voluntary associations, and evaluated by the American Council on Education; credit upon transfer from other institutions; demonstrated experiential learning (life and occupational experiences); military educational experiences evaluated by the American Council on Education

5. **Credit for successful completion of standardized achievement tests:** College-Level Examination Program (CLEP) General Examinations (Humanities examinations only), College-Level Examination Program (CLEP) Subject Examinations, College Board Advanced Placement Examinations

6. **Number of credit hours required for degree:** Associate, 60 semester hours; Bachelor, 120 semester hours

7. **Minimum campus time:** None

8. **Instructional methods provided for off-campus learning:** Correspondence courses, television courses, guided instruction via telephone and mail, cooperative education, supervised field work, sponsored experiential learning

9. **Student support services provided:** Academic advising, financial aid, orientation, counseling and testing, job placement assistance, career counseling

10. **Available informational materials:** Student handbook of pertinent policies and procedures, program catalog, program brochure

11. **Grading system:** A, B, C, D, F, or other variation of scale using A, B, C; also, four elective courses may be taken on a pass/fail basis in the associate program and eight in the bachelor program

12. **Enrollment:** 350

13. **Degrees conferred:** 138

14. **Year begun:** 1977

15. **Out-of-state students:** Accepted; tuition higher than for in-state students except for correspondence courses and for credits earned via prior learning portfolio

Indiana University Southeast

External Degree Program
Division of Continuing Studies
4201 Grant Line Road
New Albany, IN 47150

1. **Degrees and areas of study:** Associate of General Studies, Bachelor of General Studies

2. **Institutional accreditation:** North Central Association of Colleges and Schools

3. **Previous education required:** High school diploma or GED equivalency

4. **Credit for prior learning:** Satisfactory completion of instruction offered by businesses, government agencies, labor unions, or professional or voluntary associations, and evaluated by the American Council on Education; credit upon

transfer from other institutions; demonstrated experiential learning (life and occupational experiences); military educational experiences evaluated by the American Council on Education

5. **Credit for successful completion of standardized achievement tests:** College-Level Examination Program (CLEP) General Examinations, College-Level Examination Program (CLEP) Subject Examinations, College Board Advanced Placement Examinations, American College Testing (ACT) Proficiency Examination Program

6. **Number of credit hours required for degree:** Associate, 60 semester hours; Bachelor, 120 semester hours

7. **Minimum campus time:** None

8. **Instructional methods provided for off-campus learning:** Correspondence courses, video cassettes, television courses, packaged course and study guides

9. **Student support services provided:** Academic advising, financial aid, orientation, counseling and testing, job placement assistance, career counseling

10. **Available informational materials:** Student handbook of pertinent policies and procedures, program catalog, program brochure, independent study by correspondence catalog, self-acquired competency regulations

11. **Grading system:** A, B, C, D, F, or other variation of scale using A, B, C

12. **Enrollment:** 560

13. **Degrees conferred:** 159

14. **Year begun:** 1975

15. **Out-of-state students:** Accepted; tuition higher than for in-state students except for correspondence courses

Indiana University-Purdue University at Indianapolis

External Degree Program
Division of Continuing Studies
State Union G-025A
1300 West Michigan Street
Indianapolis, IN 46202

1. **Degrees and areas of study:** Associate of General Studies, Bachelor of General Studies

2. **Institutional accreditation:** North Central Association of Colleges and Schools

3. **Previous education required:** High school diploma or GED equivalency

4. **Credit for prior learning:** Satisfactory completion of instruction offered by businesses, government agencies, labor unions, or professional or voluntary associations, and evaluated by the American Council on Education; credit upon transfer from other institutions; demonstrated experiential learning (life and occupational experiences); military educational experiences evaluated by the American Council on Education

5. **Credit for successful completion of standardized achievement tests:** College-Level Examination Program (CLEP) General Examinations, College-Level Examination Program (CLEP) Subject Examinations, College Board Advanced Placement Examinations, DANTES Subject Standardized Tests (DSST)

6. **Number of credit hours required for degree:** Associate, 60 semester hours; Bachelor, 120 semester hours

7. **Minimum campus time:** None

8. **Instructional methods provided for off-campus learning:** Correspondence courses, video cassettes, television courses, newspaper courses, guided instruction via telephone and mail, packaged course and study guides, cooperative education

9. **Student support services provided:** Academic advising, financial aid, orientation, counseling and testing, job placement assistance

10. **Available informational materials:** Student handbook of pertinent policies and procedures, program catalog, program brochure, independent study by correspondence brochure

11. **Grading system:** A, B, C, D, F, or other variation of scale using A, B, C. Also, a student may elect to complete 24 semester hours of electives on a pass/fail basis. Self-Acquired Competency credit is recorded with a notation of S for satisfactory

12. **Enrollment:** 307

13. **Degrees conferred:** 153

14. **Year begun:** 1976

15. **Out-of-state students:** Accepted; tuition higher than for in-state students except for correspondence courses

Saint Mary-of-the-Woods College

Women's External Degree Program
Saint Mary-of-the-Woods, IN 47876

1. **Degrees and areas of study:** Associate of Arts or Associate of Science in: Business, Gerontology or Humanities; Bachelor of Arts or Bachelor of Science in: business, history, English, humanities, psychology, social work, religion, journalism, liberal arts; in addition, concentrations or specially designed studies available in art, creative-writing, philosophy, sociology, and translator training

2. **Institutional accreditation:** North Central Association of Colleges and Schools

3. **Previous education required:** High school diploma or GED equivalent

4. **Credit for prior learning:** Satisfactory completion of instruction offered by businesses, government agencies, labor unions, or professional or voluntary associations, and evaluated by the American Council on Education; credit upon transfer from other institutions; demonstrated experiential learning (life and occupational experiences); military educational experiences evaluated by the American Council on Education

5. **Credit for successful completion of standardized achievement tests:** College-

Level Examination Program (CLEP) General Examinations, College-Level Examination Program (CLEP) Subject Examinations

6. **Number of credit hours required for degree:** Associate, 60 semester hours; Bachelor, 122 semester hours

7. **Minimum campus time:** Three or four days of orientation; one to one and one-half days every five months thereafter

8. **Instructional methods provided for off-campus learning:** Guided instruction via telephone and mail, packaged course and study guides, supervised field work, sponsored experiential learning

9. **Student support services provided:** Academic advising, financial aid, orientation, counseling and testing, career counseling job placement assistance

10. **Available informational materials:** Student handbook of pertinent policies and procedures, program brochure, Women's External Degree Prospectus, and three other preenrollment brochures

11. **Grading system:** A, B, C, D, F, or other variation of scale using A, B, C, and pass/fail, credit/no credit, or other variation of this scale

12. **Enrollment:** 358

13. **Degrees conferred:** 449

14. **Year begun:** 1973

15. **Out-of-state students:** Accepted; tuition same as for in-state students

University of Evansville

External Studies Program
P. O. Box 329
Evansville, IN 47712

1. **Degrees and areas of study:** Bachelor of Arts, Bachelor of Science (individually designed studies)

2. **Institutional accreditation:** North Central Association of Colleges and Schools

3. **Previous education required:** High school diploma or GED equivalent

4. **Credit for prior learning:** Satisfactory completion of instruction offered by businesses, government agencies, labor unions, or professional or voluntary associations, and evaluated by the American Council on Education; credit upon transfer from other institutions; demonstrated experiential learning (life and occupational experiences); military educational experiences evaluated by the American Council on Education

5. **Credit for successful completion of standardized achievement tests:** College-Level Examination Program (CLEP) General Examinations, College-Level Examination Program (CLEP) Subject Examinations, DANTES Subject Standardized Tests (DSST)

6. **Number of credit hours required for degree:** 182 quarter hours

7. **Minimum campus time:** A two-day educational planning workshop

8. **Instructional methods provided for off-campus learning:** Guided instruction via telephone and mail, sponsored experiential learning

9. **Student support services provided:** Academic advising, financial aid, orientation, counseling and testing, career counseling job placement assistance

10. **Available informational materials:** Program brochure

11. **Grading system:** There is no predominant grading system; type of evaluation varies according to agreement between student and advisor/mentor/instructor

12. **Enrollment:** 76

13. **Degrees conferred:** 33

14. **Year begun:** 1974

15. **Out-of-state students:** Accepted; tuition same as for in-state students

Iowa State University

Bachelor of Liberal Studies Program
College of Sciences and Humanities
Ames, IA 50011

1. **Degrees and areas of study:** Bachelor of Liberal Studies (BLS). The student chooses three of the following five distribution areas: (1) Humanities, (2) Communications and Arts, (3) Natural Sciences and mathematical disciplines, (4) Social sciences, (5) Professional fields approved by the university

2. **Institutional accreditation:** North Central Association of Colleges and Schools

3. **Previous education required:** 2 years of college (62 semester hours or 93 quarter hours)

4. **Credit for prior learning:** Credit upon transfer from other institutions; military educational experiences evaluated by the American Council on Education

5. **Credit for successful completion of standardized achievement tests:** College-Level Examination Program (CLEP) General Examinations, College-Level Examination Program (CLEP) Subject Examinations

6. **Number of credit hours required for degree:** 124 semester hours or 186 quarter hours

7. **Minimum campus time:** None

8. **Instructional methods provided for off-campus learning:** Video cassettes, television courses, newspaper courses, guided instruction via telephone and mail, packaged course and study guides, supervised field work, sponsored experiential learning

9. **Student support services provided:** Academic advising, financial aid, orientation, job placement assistance

10. **Available informational materials:** Student handbook of pertinent policies and procedures, program catalog, program brochure

11. **Grading system:** A, B, C, D, F, or other variation of scale using A, B, C

12. **Enrollment:** 75

13. **Degrees conferred:** 12

14. **Year begun:** 1977

15. **Out-of-state students:** Accepted only if substantial amount of previous work is credited by Iowa Regents universities (Iowa State University, the University of Iowa, University of Northern Iowa); for most out-of-state students there is no practical way to complete the program

Kirkwood Community College

6301 Kirkwood Blvd. S.W.
P. O. Box 2068
Cedar Rapids, IA 52406

1. **Degrees and areas of study:** Associate of General Studies
2. **Institutional accreditation:** North Central Association of Colleges and Secondary Schools
3. **Previous education required:** High school diploma or GED equivalent
4. **Credit for prior learning:** Satisfactory completion of instruction offered by businesses, government agencies, labor unions, or professional or voluntary associations, and evaluated by the American Council on Education; credit upon transfer from other institutions; demonstrated experiential learning (life and occupational experiences); military educational experiences evaluated by the American Council on Education
5. **Credit for successful completion of standardized achievement tests:** College-Level Examination Program (CLEP) General Examinations, College-Level Examination Program (CLEP) Subject Examinations
6. **Number of credit hours required for degree:** 90 quarter hours
7. **Minimum campus time:** None
8. **Instructional methods provided for off-campus learning:** Video cassettes, television courses, computer-assisted, self-paced instruction, packaged course and study guides, cooperative education, supervised field work, sponsored experiential learning
9. **Student support services provided:** Academic advising, financial aid, orientation, counseling and testing, job placement assistance, career counseling
10. **Available informational materials:** Student handbook of pertinent policies and procedures, guide for portfolio development
11. **Grading system:** A, B, C, D, F, or other variation of scale using A, B, C
12. **Enrollment:** 42
13. **Degrees conferred:** 40 (estimated)
14. **Year begun:** 1977
15. **Out-of-state students:** Accepted; tuition same as for in-state students

University of Iowa

The College of Liberal Arts
Iowa City, IA 52242

1. **Degrees and areas of study:** Bachelor of Liberal Studies
2. **Institutional accreditation:** North Central Association of Colleges and Schools

3. **Previous education required:** 62 semester hours of credit and 2.0 grade point average (on 4.0 scale)

4. **Credit for prior learning:** Satisfactory completion of instruction offered by businesses, government agencies, labor unions, or professional or voluntary associations, and evaluated by the American Council on Education; credit upon transfer from other institutions; military educational experiences evaluated by the American Council on Education

5. **Credit for successful completion of standardized achievement tests:** College-Level Examination Program (CLEP) General Examinations, College-Level Examination Program (CLEP) Subject Examinations, College Board Advanced Placement Examinations, DANTES Subject Standardized Tests (DSST)

6. **Number of credit hours required for degree:** 124 semester hours

7. **Minimum campus time:** None

8. **Instructional methods provided for off-campus learning:** Correspondence courses, television courses, the "telebridge" system, which is similar to a conference telephone call, allows for class discussion among an instructor and students located at various sites around the state

9. **Student support services provided:** Academic advising, financial aid, orientation, counseling and testing, career counseling, job placement assistance

10. **Available informational materials:** Student handbook of pertinent policies and procedures, program catalog, program brochure

11. **Grading system:** A, B, C, D, F, or other variation of scale using A, B, C

12. **Enrollment:** 274

13. **Degrees conferred:** 37

14. **Year begun:** 1977

15. **Out-of-state students:** Accepted; tuition same as for in-state students

University of Northern Iowa

Bachelor of Liberal Studies Program
23rd and College
Cedar Falls, IA 50614

1. **Degrees and areas of study:** Bachelor of Liberal Studies

2. **Institutional accreditation:** North Central Association of Colleges and Schools

3. **Previous education required:** 2 years of college (62 semester hours or 93 quarter hours)

4. **Credit for prior learning:** Satisfactory completion of instruction offered by businesses, government agencies, labor unions, or professional or voluntary associations, and evaluated by the American Council on Education; credit upon transfer from other institutions; military educational experiences evaluated by the American Council on Education

5. **Credit for successful completion of standardized achievement tests:** College-Level Examination Program (CLEP) General Examinations, College-Level Examination Program (CLEP) Subject Examinations, College Board Advanced Placement Examinations, American College Testing (ACT) Proficiency Examination Program, DANTES Subject Standardized Tests (DSST)

6. **Number of credit hours required for degree:** 124 semester hours

7. **Minimum campus time:** None

8. **Instructional methods provided for off-campus learning:** Correspondence courses, television courses, newspaper courses

9. **Student support services provided:** Academic advising, financial aid, counseling and testing, career counseling, job placement assistance

10. **Available informational materials:** Student handbook of pertinent policies and procedures, program brochure, the regular university catalog, correspondence course brochure, and other descriptive material and charts

11. **Grading system:** A, B, C, D, F, or other variation of scale using A, B, C

12. **Enrollment:** 80

13. **Degrees conferred:** 33

14. **Year begun:** 1977

15. **Out-of-state students:** Accepted, if former University of Northern Iowa students; tuition for correspondence study is the same for both in-state and out-of-state students

Upper Iowa University

Coordinated Off-Campus Degree Program
Fayette, IA 52142

1. **Degrees and areas of study:** Bachelor of Arts in Public Administration, Business Administration

2. **Institutional accreditation:** North Central Association of Colleges and Schools

3. **Previous education required:** High school diploma or GED equivalent

4. **Credit for prior learning:** Satisfactory completion of instruction offered by businesses, government agencies, labor unions, or professional or voluntary associations, and evaluated by the American Council on Education; credit upon transfer from other institutions; demonstrated experiential learning (life and occupational experiences); military educational experiences evaluated by the American Council on Education

5. **Credit for successful completion of standardized achievement tests:** College-Level Examination Program (CLEP) Subject Examinations, American College Testing (ACT) Proficiency Examination Program, DANTES Subject Standardized Tests (DSST)

6. **Number of credit hours required for degree:** 124 semester hours

7. **Minimum campus time:** Two to four weeks of campus residency required; student completes four semester hours (2 weeks) or seven semester hours (4 weeks)

8. **Instructional methods provided for off-campus learning:** Correspondence courses, guided instruction via telephone and mail, packaged course and study guides

9. **Student support services provided:** Academic advising, financial aid

10. **Available informational materials:** Program catalog, program brochure

11. **Grading system:** A, B, C, D, F, or other variation of scale using A, B, C

12. **Enrollment:** Public Administration, 449; Business Administration, 1,541

13. **Degrees conferred:** Public Administration, 340 (estimated); Business Administration, 680 (estimated)

14. **Year begun:** Public Administration, 1973; Business Administration, 1974

15. **Out-of-state students:** Accepted; tuition same as for in-state students

Dodge City Community College

Outreach and External Studies Program
14th Avenue and Highway 50 By-pass
Dodge City, KS 67801

1. **Degrees and areas of study:** Associate of Arts
2. **Institutional accreditation:** North Central Association of Colleges and Schools
3. **Previous education required:** High school diploma or GED equivalent
4. **Credit for prior learning:** Credit upon transfer from other institutions
5. **Credit for successful completion of standardized achievement tests:** College-Level Examination Program (CLEP) Subject Examinations
6. **Number of credit hours required for degree:** 62 semester hours
7. **Minimum campus time:** None
8. **Instructional methods provided for off-campus learning:** Video cassettes, television courses, guided instruction via telephone and mail, packaged course and study guides
9. **Student support services provided:** Academic advising, counseling and testing, career counseling, job placement assistance
10. **Available informational materials:** Program brochure
11. **Grading system:** A, B, C, D, F, or other variation of scale using A, B, C
12. **Enrollment:** 150
13. **Degrees conferred:** Cannot be estimated
14. **Year begun:** 1973
15. **Out-of-state students:** not accepted

Donnelly College

Person-Centered Degree Program, Guided Study
608 North 18th Street
Kansas City, KS 66102

1. **Degrees and areas of study:** Associate of Arts
2. **Institutional accreditation:** North Central Association of Colleges and Schools
3. **Previous education required:** High school diploma or GED equivalent
4. **Credit for prior learning:** Satisfactory completion of instruction offered by businesses, government agencies, labor unions, or professional or voluntary associations, and evaluated by the American Council on Education; credit upon

transfer from other institutions; demonstrated experiential learning (life and occupational experiences); military educational experiences evaluated by the American Council on Education

5. **Credit for successful completion of standardized achievement tests:** College-Level Examination Program (CLEP) General Examinations, College-Level Examination Program (CLEP) Subject Examinations, College Board Advanced Placement Examinations, American College Testing (ACT) Proficiency Examination Program

6. **Number of credit hours required for degree:** 64 semester hours

7. **Minimum campus time:** None

8. **Instructional methods provided for off-campus learning:** Correspondence courses, video cassettes, guided instruction via telephone and mail, computer-assisted, self-paced instruction, packaged course and study guides

9. **Student support services provided:** Academic advising, financial aid, orientation, counseling and testing, career counseling, job placement assistance

10. **Available informational materials:** Student handbook of pertinent policies and procedures

11. **Grading system:** A, B, C, D, F, or other variation of scale using A, B, C

12. **Enrollment:** 55

13. **Degrees conferred:** None

14. **Year begun:** 1975

15. **Out-of-state students:** Accepted; tuition same as for in-state students

Kansas State University

Nontraditional Study Program
313 Umberger Hall
Manhattan, KS 66502

1. **Degrees and areas of study:** Bachelor of Arts, Bachelor of Science (selected major areas of study)

2. **Institutional accreditation:** North Central Association of Colleges and Schools

3. **Previous education required:** High school diploma or GED equivalent

4. **Credit for prior learning:** Credit upon transfer from other institutions; demonstrated experiential learning (life and occupational experiences); military educational experiences evaluated by the American Council on Education

5. **Credit for successful completion of standardized achievement tests:** College-Level Examination Program (CLEP) General Examinations, College-Level Examination Program (CLEP) Subject Examinations, American College Testing (ACT) Proficiency Examination Program, College Board Advanced Placement Examinations, DANTES Subject Standardized Tests (DSST)

6. **Number of credit hours required for degree:** 120, 124, 128 semester hours (depending on degree program)

7. **Minimum campus time:** None
8. **Instructional methods provided for off-campus learning:** Correspondence courses, television courses, newspaper courses, guided instruction via telephone and mail, packaged course and study guides, supervised field work, sponsored experiential learning
9. **Student support services provided:** Academic advising, financial aid, orientation, career counseling
10. **Available informational materials:** Student handbook of pertinent policies and procedures, program brochure, semester schedules, Regents independent study guide, credit by examination brochure
11. **Grading system:** A, B, C, D, F, or other variation of scale using A, B, C, and pass/fail, credit/no credit, or other variation of this scale
12. **Enrollment:** 180
13. **Degrees conferred:** 30 (estimated)
14. **Year begun:** 1975
15. **Out-of-state students:** Not accepted

Saint Joseph's College

External Degree Programs
North Windham, ME 04062

1. **Degrees and areas of study:** Bachelor of Science in Business Administration; Bachelor of Science in Health Care Administration; Bachelor of Science in Professional Arts

2. **Institutional accreditation:** New England Association of Schools and Colleges

3. **Previous education required:** High school diploma or GED equivalency for all programs; for the Bachelor of Science in Professional Arts, an R.N. diploma or associate degree is necessary

4. **Credit for prior learning:** Satisfactory completion of instruction offered by businesses, government agencies, labor unions, or professional or voluntary associations, and evaluated by the American Council on Education; credit upon transfer from other institutions; military educational experiences evaluated by the American Council on Education

5. **Credit for successful completion of standardized achievement tests:** College-Level Examination Program (CLEP) General Examinations, College-Level Examination Program (CLEP) Subject Examinations, DANTES Subject Standardized Tests (DSST)

6. **Number of credit hours required for degree:** 128 semester hours

7. **Minimum campus time:** One three-week residency period during the summer for nine (9) semester hours of credit

8. **Instructional methods provided for off-campus learning:** Guided instruction via telephone and mail, packaged course and study guides

9. **Student support services provided:** Academic advising, financial aid, orientation, counseling and testing

10. **Available informational materials:** Student handbook of pertinent policies and procedures, program catalog, newsletter

11. **Grading system:** A, B, C, D, F, or other variation of scale using A, B, C

12. **Enrollment:** Bachelor of Science in Business Administration and Bachelor of Science in Health Care Administration, 950; Bachelor of Science in Professional Arts, 5,500

13. **Degrees conferred:** Bachelor of Science in Business Administration and Bachelor of Science in Health Care Administration, 0; Bachelor of Science in Professional Arts, 675

14. **Year begun:** Bachelor of Science in Business Administration and Bachelor of Science in Health Care Administration, 1982; Bachelor of Science in Professional Arts, 1976

15. **Out-of-state students:** Accepted; tuition same as for in-state students

Columbia Union College

External Studies Program
7600 Flower Avenue
Takoma Park, MD 20912

1. **Degrees and areas of study:** Associate of Liberal Studies; Bachelor of Liberal Studies

2. **Institutional accreditation:** Middle States Association of Colleges and Schools

3. **Previous education required:** High school diploma or GED equivalent

4. **Credit for prior learning:** Credit upon transfer from other institutions; demonstrated experiential learning (life and occupational experiences)

5. **Credit for successful completion of standardized achievement tests:** College-Level Examination Program (CLEP) General Examinations, College-Level Examination Program (CLEP) Subject Examinations, College Board Advanced Placement Examinations, American College Testing (ACT) Proficiency Examination Program

6. **Number of credit hours required for degree:** Associate, 64 semester hours; bachelor, 128 semester hours

7. **Minimum campus time:** None

8. **Instructional methods provided for off-campus learning:** Correspondence courses, packaged course and study guides

9. **Student support services provided:** Academic advising, orientation, counseling and testing

10. **Available informational materials:** Student handbook of pertinent policies and procedures, program catalog, program brochure

11. **Grading system:** A, B, C, D, F, or other variation of scale using A, B, C

12. **Enrollment:** 100

13. **Degrees conferred:** 12

14. **Year begun:** 1975

15. **Out-of-state students:** Accepted; tuition same as for in-state students

University of Maryland

University College
University Boulevard at Adelphi Road
College Park, MD 20742

1. **Degrees and areas of study:** Bachelor of Arts, Bachelor of Science (with selected major area of concentration)

43

2. **Institutional accreditation:** Middle States Association of Colleges and Schools

3. **Previous education required:** High school diploma or GED equivalent

4. **Credit for prior learning:** Satisfactory completion of instruction offered by businesses, government agencies, labor unions, or professional or voluntary associations, and evaluated by the American Council on Education; credit upon transfer from other institutions; demonstrated experiential learning (life and occupational experiences); military educational experiences evaluated by the American Council on Education

5. **Credit for successful completion of standardized achievement tests:** College-Level Examination Program. (CLEP) General Examinations, College-Level Examination Program (CLEP) Subject Examinations, American College Testing (ACT) Proficiency Examination Program, DANTES Subject Standardized Tests (DSST), College Board Advanced Placement Examinations

6. **Number of credit hours required for degree:** 120 semester hours

7. **Minimum campus time:** None

8. **Instructional methods provided for off-campus learning:** Video cassettes, television courses, newspaper courses, guided instruction via telephone and mail, packaged course and study guides, cooperative education, supervised field work

9. **Student support services provided:** Academic advising, financial aid, orientation, counseling and testing, career counseling, job placement assistance

10. **Available informational materials:** Program catalog.

11. **Grading system:** A, B, C, D, F, or other variation of scale using A, B, C

12. **Enrollment:** 65,452 (includes associate degrees offered overseas)

13. **Degrees conferred:** 25,377 (Bachelor of Arts, Bachelor of Science)

14. **Year begun:** 1947

15. **Out-of-state students:** Accepted within state that is authorized to offer courses; tuition same as for in-state students

Atlantic Union College

The Adult Degree Program
Main Street
South Lancaster, MA 01567

1. **Degrees and areas of study:** Bachelor of Arts
2. **Institutional accreditation:** New England Association of Schools and Colleges
3. **Previous education required:** High school diploma or GED equivalent
4. **Credit for prior learning:** Satisfactory completion of instruction offered by businesses, government agencies, labor unions, or professional or voluntary associations, and evaluated by the American Council on Education; credit upon transfer from other institutions; demonstrated experiential learning (life and occupational experiences); military educational experiences evaluated by the American Council on Education
5. **Credit for successful completion of standardized achievement tests:** College-Level Examination Program (CLEP) General Examinations, College-Level Examination Program (CLEP) Subject Examinations
6. **Number of credit hours required for degree:** 128 semester hours
7. **Minimum campus time:** Two-week seminars at six-month intervals
8. **Instructional methods provided for off-campus learning:** Guided instruction via telephone and mail, packaged course and study guides, cooperative education, supervised field work, sponsored experiential learning
9. **Student support services provided:** Academic advising, financial aid, orientation, counseling and testing, career counseling, job placement assistance
10. **Available informational materials:** Program brochure
11. **Grading system:** Pass/fail, credit/no credit, or other variation of this scale
12. **Enrollment:** 65
13. **Degrees conferred:** 180 (estimated)
14. **Year begun:** 1972
15. **Out-of-state students:** Accepted; tuition same as for in-state students

Ferris State College

School of Allied Health
Big Rapids, MI 49307

1. **Degrees and areas of study:** Bachelor of Science in Environmental Health, Bachelor of Science in Health Services Management

2. **Institutional accreditation:** North Central Association of Colleges and Schools

3. **Previous education required:** High school diploma or GED equivalent or a demonstrated ability to function academically at the collegiate level and a year of experience in a field related to the degree

4. **Credit for prior learning:** Satisfactory completion of instruction offered by businesses, government agencies, labor unions, or professional or voluntary associations, and evaluated by the American Council on Education; credit upon transfer from other institutions; demonstrated experiential learning (life and occupational experiences); military educational experiences evaluated by the American Council on Education

5. **Credit for successful completion of standardized achievement tests:** College-Level Examination Program (CLEP) General Examinations, College-Level Examination Program (CLEP) Subject Examinations, American College Testing (ACT) Proficiency Examination Program

6. **Number of credit hours required for degree:** Bachelor of Science in Environmental Health, 180 quarter hours; Bachelor of Science in Health Services Management, 182 quarter hours

7. **Minimum campus time:** Bachelor of Science in Environmental Health, a single short-term summer session not required but suggested; Bachelor of Science in Health Services Management, none

8. **Instructional methods provided for off-campus learning:** Bachelor of Science in Environmental Health, correspondence courses, guided instruction via telephone and mail, packaged course and study guides, cooperative education, supervised field work, sponsored experiential learning; Bachelor of Science in Health Services Management, guided instruction via telephone and mail, cooperative education, supervised field work, sponsored experiential learning

9. **Student support services provided:** Academic advising, orientation, counseling and testing, job placement assistance

10. **Available informational materials:** Program catalog, program brochure, guidelines for formal portfolio development, postadmission information packet

11. **Grading system:** A, B, C, D, F, or other variation of scale using A, B, C

12. **Enrollment:** Bachelor of Science in Environmental Health, 100; Bachelor of Science in Health Services Management, 50

13. **Degrees conferred:** Bachelor of Science in Environmental Health, 6 (estimated); Bachelor of Science in Health Services Management, none
14. **Year begun:** Bachelor of Science in Environmental Health, 1978; Bachelor of Science in Health Services Management, 1981
15. **Out-of-state students:** Bachelor of Science in Environmental Health, accepted, tuition same as for in-state students; Bachelor of Science in Health Services Management, not accepted

Northwood Institute

External Plan of Study Program
3225 Cook Road
Midland, MI 48640

1. **Degrees and areas of study:** Bachelor of Business Administration
2. **Institutional accreditation:** North Central Association of Colleges and Schools
3. **Previous education required:** High school diploma or GED equivalent
4. **Credit for prior learning:** Satisfactory completion of instruction offered by businesses, government agencies, labor unions, or professional or voluntary associations, and evaluated by the American Council on Education; credit upon transfer from other institutions; demonstrated experiential learning (life and occupational experiences); military educational experiences evaluated by the American Council on Education
5. **Credit for successful completion of standardized achievement tests:** College-Level Examination Program (CLEP) General Examinations, College-Level Examination Program (CLEP) Subject Examinations, American College Testing (ACT) Proficiency Examination Program, College Board Advanced Placement Examinations, DANTES Subject Standardized Tests (DSST)
6. **Number of credit hours required for degree:** 180 quarter hours
7. **Minimum campus time:** Two three-day seminars; one several-hour block of time for a comprehensive oral examination with a faculty committee
8. **Instructional methods provided for off-campus learning:** Correspondence courses, guided instruction via telephone and mail, packaged course and study guides, cooperative education, supervised field work, sponsored experiential learning
9. **Student support services provided:** Academic advising, financial aid, orientation, counseling and testing, career counseling, job placement assistance
10. **Available informational materials:** Students receive a packet of information and directions
11. **Grading system:** A, B, C, D, F, or other variation of scale using A, B, C
12. **Enrollment:** 655
13. **Degrees conferred:** 375 (estimated)
14. **Year begun:** 1966
15. **Out-of-state students:** Accepted; tuition same as for in-state students

Wayne State University

University Studies/Weekend College Program
6001 Cass Avenue
Detroit, MI 48202

1. **Degrees and areas of study:** Bachelor of General Studies
2. **Institutional accreditation:** North Central Association of Colleges and Schools
3. **Previous education required:** High school diploma or GED equivalent
4. **Credit for prior learning:** Satisfactory completion of instruction offered by businesses, government agencies, labor unions, or professional or voluntary associations, and evaluated by the American Council on Education; credit upon transfer from other institutions; military educational experiences evaluated by the American Council on Education
5. **Credit for successful completion of standardized achievement tests:** College-Level Examination Program (CLEP) General Examinations, College-Level Examination Program (CLEP) Subject Examinations, College Board Advanced Placement Examinations, DANTES Subject Standardized Tests (DSST)
6. **Number of credit hours required for degree:** 120 semester hours
7. **Minimum campus time:** While there is no minimum as a matter of policy, as a matter of practical scheduling, it would be very inconvenient to avoid a certain number of 4-semester-hour weekend courses; around 20 semester hours would be a practical minimum
8. **Instructional methods provided for off-campus learning:** Video cassettes, television courses, packaged course and study guides, supervised field work, sponsored experiential learning
9. **Student support services provided:** Academic advising, financial aid, orientation, counseling and testing, career counseling
10. **Available informational materials:** Program catalog, program brochure
11. **Grading system:** A, B, C, D, F, or other variation of scale using A, B, C
12. **Enrollment:** 750
13. **Degrees conferred:** 1,100 (estimated)
14. **Year begun:** 1974
15. **Out-of-state students:** Accepted; tuition higher than for in-state students

Western Michigan University

Division of Continuing Education
W. Michigan Avenue
Kalamazoo, MI 49008

1. **Degrees and areas of study:** Bachelor of Arts or Bachelor of Science in American studies, applied liberal studies, environmental studies, health studies, social science studies, technical scientific studies

2. **Institutional accreditation:** North Central Association of Colleges and Schools
3. **Previous education required:** One to two years of college or an approved professional license or credential
4. **Credit for prior learning:** Credit upon transfer from other institutions; demonstrated experiential learning (life and occupational experiences)
5. **Credit for successful completion of standardized achievement tests:** College-Level Examination Program (CLEP) General Examinations, College-Level Examination Program (CLEP) Subject Examinations, College Board Advanced Placement Examinations
6. **Number of credit hours required for degree:** 122 semester hours
7. **Minimum campus time:** None
8. **Instructional methods provided for off-campus learning:** Correspondence courses, video cassettes, television courses, newspaper courses, sponsored experiential learning
9. **Student support services provided:** Academic advising, financial aid, counseling and testing, career counseling, job placement assistance
10. **Available informational materials:** Program brochure
11. **Grading system:** A, B, C, D, F, or other variation of scale using A, B, C
12. **Enrollment:** 650
13. **Degrees conferred:** 700
14. **Year begun:** 1973
15. **Out-of-state students:** Accepted; tuition higher than for in-state students

Bemidji State University

External Studies Program
Bemidji, MN 56601

1. **Degrees and areas of study:** Associate of Arts, Associate of Science, Bachelor of Arts, Bachelor of Science (selected majors)

2. **Institutional accreditation:** North Central Association of Colleges and Schools

3. **Previous education required:** High school diploma or GED equivalent

4. **Credit for prior learning:** Satisfactory completion of instruction offered by businesses, government agencies, labor unions, or professional or voluntary associations, and evaluated by the American Council on Education; credit upon transfer from other institutions; demonstrated experiential learning (life and occupational experiences); military educational experiences evaluated by the American Council on Education

5. **Credit for successful completion of standardized achievement tests:** College-Level Examination Program (CLEP) General Examinations, College-Level Examination Program (CLEP) Subject Examinations, American College Testing (ACT) Proficiency Examination Program, College Board Advanced Placement Examinations, DANTES Subject Standardized Tests (DSST)

6. **Number of credit hours required for degree:** Associate of Arts, Associate of Science, 96 quarter hours; Bachelor of Arts, 180 quarter hours; Bachelor of Science, 192 quarter hours

7. **Minimum campus time:** None

8. **Instructional methods provided for off-campus learning:** Correspondence courses, video cassettes, television courses, guided instruction via telephone and mail, packaged course and study guides

9. **Student support services provided:** Academic advising, financial aid, counseling and testing, job placement assistance

10. **Available informational materials:** Student handbook of pertinent policies and procedures, program catalog, program brochure, newsletters

11. **Grading system:** A, B, C, D, F, or other variation of scale using A, B, C

12. **Enrollment:** 900

13. **Degrees conferred:** 200 (estimated)

14. **Year begun:** 1973

15. **Out-of-state students:** Accepted; tuition higher than for in-state students

College of St. Scholastica

ENCORE Program
1200 Kenwood Avenue
Duluth, MN 55811

1. **Degrees and areas of study:** Bachelor of Arts. An ENCORE student may choose a course of study in any one of the college's more than 40 areas of concentration or design an individually planned major in career-oriented fields such as management or nursing

2. **Institutional accreditation:** North Central Association of Colleges and Schools

3. **Previous education required:** High school diploma or GED equivalent

4. **Credit for prior learning:** Satisfactory completion of instruction offered by businesses, government agencies, labor unions, or professional or voluntary associations, and evaluated by the American Council on Education; credit upon transfer from other institutions; demonstrated experiential learning (life and occupational experiences); military educational experiences evaluated by the American Council on Education

5. **Credit for successful completion of standardized achievement tests:** College-Level Examination Program (CLEP) General Examinations, College-Level Examination Program (CLEP) Subject Examinations, College Board Advanced Placement Examinations

6. **Number of credit hours required for degree:** 192 quarter hours, 42 of which must be taken under the auspices of the college faculty. Of these 42, 16 must be earned at the college's internship program—Direct Action Program (DAP)

7. **Minimum campus time:** None

8. **Instructional methods provided for off-campus learning:** Television courses, newspaper courses, guided instruction via telephone and mail, cooperative education, supervised field work, sponsored experiential learning

9. **Student support services provided:** Academic advising, financial aid, orientation, counseling and testing, career counseling, job placement assistance

10. **Available informational materials:** Student handbook of pertinent policies and procedures, program catalog, program brochure

11. **Grading system:** A, B, C, D, F, or other variation of scale using A, B, C

12. **Enrollment:** 200

13. **Degrees conferred:** 0

14. **Year begun:** 1980

15. **Out-of-state students:** Accepted; tuition same as for in-state students

Lakewood Community College

3401 Century Avenue
White Bear Lake, MN 55110

1. **Degrees and areas of study:** Associate Degree
2. **Institutional accreditation:** North Central Association of Colleges and Schools
3. **Previous education required:** High school diploma or GED equivalent
4. **Credit for prior learning:** Satisfactory completion of instruction offered by businesses, government agencies, labor unions, or professional or voluntary associations, and evaluated by the American Council on Education; credit upon transfer from other institutions; demonstrated experiential learning (life and occupational experiences); military educational experiences evaluated by the American Council on Education
5. **Credit for successful completion of standardized achievement tests:** College-Level Examination Program (CLEP) General Examinations, College-Level Examination Program (CLEP) Subject Examinations, American College Testing (ACT) Proficiency Examination Program, College Board Advanced Placement Examinations, DANTES Subject Standardized Tests (DSST)
6. **Number of credit hours required for degree:** 90 quarter hours
7. **Minimum campus time:** None
8. **Instructional methods provided for off-campus learning:** Guided instruction via telephone and mail, packaged course and study guides, cooperative education, supervised field work, sponsored experiential learning
9. **Student support services provided:** Academic advising, financial aid, orientation, counseling and testing, career counseling
10. **Available informational materials:** Student handbook of pertinent policies and procedures, program catalog, program brochure
11. **Grading system:** A, B, C, D, F, or other variation of scale using A, B, C, and pass/fail, credit/no credit, or other variation of this scale
12. **Enrollment:** 350
13. **Degrees conferred:** 300
14. **Year begun:** 1975
15. **Out-of-state students:** Accepted; tuition higher than for in-state students

Moorhead State University

External Studies Program
1104 Seventh Avenue, South
Moorhead, MN 56560

1. **Degrees and areas of study:** Bachelor of Arts, Bachelor of Science (individually designed studies and traditional majors)

2. **Institutional accreditation:** North Central Association of Colleges and Schools

3. **Previous education required:** High school diploma or GED equivalent

4. **Credit for prior learning:** Credit upon transfer from other institutions; demonstrated experiential learning (life and occupational experiences); military educational experiences evaluated by the American Council on Education

5. **Credit for successful completion of standardized achievement tests:** College-Level Examination Program (CLEP) Subject Examinations

6. **Number of credit hours required for degree:** 192 quarter hours

7. **Minimum campus time:** Varies according to major

8. **Instructional methods provided for off-campus learning:** Television courses, guided instruction via telephone and mail, packaged course and study guides, cooperative education, supervised field work, sponsored experiential learning

9. **Student support services provided:** Academic advising, financial aid, orientation, counseling and testing, career counseling, job placement assistance

10. **Available informational materials:** Student handbook of pertinent policies and procedures, program brochure, information on packaged courses

11. **Grading system:** A, B, C, D, F, or other variation of scale using A, B, C

12. **Enrollment:** 1,265

13. **Degrees conferred:** 166

14. **Year begun:** 1973

15. **Out-of-state students:** Wisconsin, North Dakota, South Dakota only; tuition same as for in-state students

Saint Mary's College

Graduate Program
Winona, MN 55987

1. **Degrees and areas of study:** Master of Arts in Educational Administration or Educational Leadership, Master of Arts in Human and Health Services Administration, Master of Arts in Counseling and Psychological Services, Master of Arts in Education, Master of Arts in Human Development

2. **Institutional accreditation:** North Central Association of Colleges and Schools

3. **Previous education required:** Bachelor's degree

4. **Credit for prior learning:** Credit upon transfer from other institutions

5. **Credit for successful completion of standardized achievement tests:** None

6. **Number of credit hours required for degree:** Master of Arts in Educational Administration or Educational Leadership, Master of Arts in Human and Health Services Administration, Master of Arts in Education, Master of Arts in Human Development, 32 semester hours; Master of Arts in Counseling and Psychological Services, 30 semester hours

7. **Minimum campus time:** Master of Arts in Educational Administration or

Educational Leadership, 12 semester credits are required during summer sessions; Master of Arts in Human and Health Services Administration, Master of Arts in Education, Master of Arts in Human Development, one week; Master of Arts in Counseling and Psychological Services, three semester credits are required during summer session

8. **Instructional methods provided for off-campus learning:** Master of Arts in Educational Administration or Educational Leadership, individual contracts with Saint Mary's College drawn up and supervised by the program director; Master of Arts in Human and Health Services Administration, computer-assisted, self-paced instruction, packaged course and study guides; Master of Arts in Counseling and Psychological Services, supervised field work, independent study course arrangements; Master of Arts in Education and Master of Arts in Human Development, individual contracts

9. **Student support services provided:** Master of Arts in Educational Administration or Educational Leadership, academic advising, financial aid, orientation, counseling and testing, career counseling, job placement assistance; Master of Arts in Human and Health Services Administration, academic advising, financial aid, orientation, career counseling, job placement assistance; Master of Arts in Counseling and Psychological Services, academic advising, financial aid, orientation, counseling and testing, career counseling, job placement assistance; Master of Arts in Education and Master of Arts in Human Development, academic advising, financial aid, orientation, career counseling, job placement assistance

10. **Available informational materials:** Master of Arts in Educational Administration or Educational Leadership and Master of Arts in Counseling and Psychological Services, program catalog, program brochure; Master of Arts in Human and Health Services Administration, none; Master of Arts in Education and Master of Arts in Human Development, student handbook of pertinent policies and procedures, program catalog, program brochure

11. **Grading system:** Master of Arts in Educational Administration or Educational Leadership, Master of Arts in Human and Health Services Administration, Master of Arts in Education and Master of Arts in Human Development, pass/fail, credit/no credit, or other variation of this scale; Master of Arts in Counseling and Psychological Services, A, B, C, D, F, or other variation of this scale using A, B, C

12. **Enrollment:** Master of Arts in Educational Administration or Educational Leadership; Master of Arts in Human and Health Services Administration, 6; Master of Arts in Counseling and Psychological Services, 80; Master of Arts in Education and Master of Arts in Human Development, 125

13. **Degrees conferred:** Master of Arts in Educational Administration or Educational Leadership, 6; Master of Arts in Human and Health Services Administration, none; Master of Arts in Counseling and Psychological Services, 100 (estimated); Master of Arts in Education and Master of Arts in Human Development, 200 (estimated)

14. **Year begun:** Master of Arts in Educational Administration or Educational Leadership, 1978; Master of Arts in Human and Health Services Administration,

1981; Master of Arts in Counseling and Psychological Services, 1982; Master of Arts in Education and Master of Arts in Human Development, 1973

15. **Out-of-state students:** Master of Arts in Educational Administration or Educational Leadership, Master of Arts in Human and Health Services Administration and Master of Arts in Counseling and Psychological Services, accepted; tuition same as for in-state students; Master of Arts in Education and Master of Arts in Human Development, accepted, tuition higher than for in-state students

University of Minnesota

Independent Study Department
47 Wesbrook Hall
77 Pleasant Street, SE
Minneapolis, MN 55455

1. **Degrees and areas of study:** Associate of Liberal Arts; Associate of Arts

2. **Institutional accreditation:** North Central Association of Colleges and Schools

3. **Previous education required:** High school diploma or GED equivalency or less, as anyone may take 39 or more quarter credits and apply for admission with a grade point average of 2.2 on a scale of 4.0

4. **Credit for prior learning:** Associate of Liberal Arts, credit upon transfer from other institutions; military educational experiences evaluated by the American Council on Education; Associate of Arts, credit upon transfer from other institutions; demonstrated experiential learning (life and occupational experiences); military educational experiences evaluated by the American Council on Education

5. **Credit for successful completion of standardized achievement tests:** College-Level Examination Program (CLEP) General Examinations

6. **Number of credit hours required for degree:** 90 quarter hours

7. **Minimum campus time:** None

8. **Instructional methods provided for off-campus learning:** Associate of Liberal Arts, correspondence courses, video cassettes, television courses, newspaper courses, guided instruction via telephone and mail, packaged course and study guides; Associate of Arts, correspondence courses, video cassettes, television courses, newspaper courses, guided instruction via telephone and mail, packaged course and study guides, sponsored experiential learning

9. **Student support services provided:** Academic advising, financial aid, counseling and testing, career counseling on campus with a fee

10. **Available informational materials:** Student handbook of pertinent policies and procedures, program catalog

11. **Grading system:** A, B, C, D, F, or other variation of scale using A, B, C

12. **Enrollment:** Information not available

13. **Degrees conferred:** Information not available

14. **Year begun:** 1958
15. **Out-of-state students:** Accepted; tuition same as for in-state students

University of Minnesota

University Without Walls
201 Wesbrook Hall
77 Pleasant Street, SE
Minneapolis, MN 55455

1. **Degrees and areas of study:** Bachelor of Arts or Bachelor of Science in individualized studies
2. **Institutional accreditation:** North Central Association of Colleges and Schools
3. **Previous education required:** Ability to demonstrate the skills required to complete the program upon application
4. **Credit for prior learning:** Satisfactory completion of instruction offered by businesses, government agencies, labor unions, or professional or voluntary associations, and evaluated by the American Council on Education; credit upon transfer from other institutions; demonstrated experiential learning (life and occupational experiences); military educational experiences evaluated by the American Council on Education
5. **Credit for successful completion of standardized achievement tests:** College-Level Examination Program (CLEP) General Examinations, College-Level Examination Program (CLEP) Subject Examinations, American College Testing (ACT) Proficiency Examination Program, College Board Advanced Placement Examinations, DANTES Subject Standardized Tests (DSST)
6. **Number of credit hours required for degree:** Credits are not used; students must satisfy the following graduation criteria: depth criteria include knowledge in an area of concentration and a major project; breadth criteria cover the liberal arts education requirement; effective written communication (in English)
7. **Minimum campus time:** None
8. **Instructional methods provided for off-campus learning:** Correspondence courses, video cassettes, television courses, newspaper courses, guided instruction via telephone and mail, computer-assisted, self-paced instruction, packaged course and study guides, cooperative education, supervised field work, sponsored experiential learning
9. **Student support services provided:** Academic advising, financial aid, orientation
10. **Available informational materials:** Student handbook of pertinent policies and procedures, program brochure, prior learning experience handbook
11. **Grading system:** There is no predominant grading system; type of evaluation varies according to agreement between student and advisor/mentor/instructor
12. **Enrollment:** 185
13. **Degrees conferred:** 316
14. **Year begun:** 1971
15. **Out-of-state students:** Accepted; tuition same as for in-state students

Winona State University

External Studies Program
Winona, MN 55987

1. **Degrees and areas of study:** Associate of Arts, Bachelor of Arts, Bachelor of Science (selected majors)
2. **Institutional accreditation:** North Central Association of Colleges and Schools
3. **Previous education required:** High school diploma or GED equivalent
4. **Credit for prior learning:** Satisfactory completion of instruction offered by businesses, government agencies, labor unions, or professional or voluntary associations, and evaluated by the American Council on Education; credit upon transfer from other institutions; demonstrated experiential learning (life and occupational experiences); military educational experiences evaluated by the American Council on Education
5. **Credit for successful completion of standardized achievement tests:** College-Level Examination Program (CLEP) General Examinations, College-Level Examination Program (CLEP) Subject Examinations, DANTES Subject Standardized Tests (DSST)
6. **Number of credit hours required for degree:** Associate, 92 quarter hours; Bachelor, 192 quarter hours
7. **Minimum campus time:** None
8. **Instructional methods provided for off-campus learning:** Video cassettes, newspaper courses, supervised field work, sponsored experiential learning
9. **Student support services provided:** Academic advising, financial aid, orientation, counseling and testing, career counseling, job placement assistance
10. **Available informational materials:** Student handbook of pertinent policies and procedures, program catalog, program brochure
11. **Grading system:** A, B, C, D, F, or other variation of scale using A, B, C
12. **Enrollment:** 1,029
13. **Degrees conferred:** 355
14. **Year begun:** 1973
15. **Out-of-state students:** Accepted; tuition higher than for in-state students

Ottawa University Kansas City

Degree Completion Program
605 West 47th Street, Suite 317
Kansas City, MO 64112

1. **Degrees and areas of study:** Bachelor of Arts (individually designed studies); Bachelor of Arts in Health Care and Administration or Health Care and Education

2. **Institutional accreditation:** North Central Association of Colleges and Schools

3. **Previous education required:** Bachelor of Arts, none; Bachelor of Arts in Health Care and Administration or Health Care and Education, the student should be an allied health professional or have significant health-care background

4. **Credit for prior learning:** Satisfactory completion of instruction offered by businesses, government agencies, labor unions, or professional or voluntary associations, and evaluated by the American Council on Education; credit upon transfer from other institutions; demonstrated experiential learning (life and occupational experiences); military educational experiences evaluated by the American Council on Education

5. **Credit for successful completion of standardized achievement tests:** College-Level Examination Program (CLEP) General Examinations, College-Level Examination Program (CLEP) Subject Examinations, DANTES Subject Standardized Tests (DSST)

6. **Number of credit hours required for degree:** 128 semester hours

7. **Minimum campus time:** Bachelor of Arts, an initial 8-week course; Bachelor of Arts in Health Care and Administration or Health Care and Education, none

8. **Instructional methods provided for off-campus learning:** Guided instruction via telephone and mail, packaged course and study guides, supervised field work

9. **Student support services provided:** Academic advising, career counseling

10. **Available informational materials:** Student handbook of pertinent policies and procedures, program catalog, program brochure

11. **Grading system:** Bachelor of Arts, A, B, C, D, F, or other variation of scale using A, B, C and pass/fail, credit/no credit, or other variation of this scale; Bachelor of Arts in Health Care and Administration or Health Care and Education, A, B, C, D, F, or other variation of scale using A, B, C

12. **Enrollment:** Bachelor of Arts, 224; Bachelor of Arts in Health Care and Administration or Health Care and Education, 220

13. **Degrees conferred:** Bachelor of Arts, 260; Bachelor of Arts in Health Care and Administration or Health Care and Education, 498

14. **Year begun:** 1974

15. **Out-of-state students:** Accepted; tuition same as for in-state students

Stephens College

School of Liberal and Professional Studies
Stephens College Without Walls
Columbia, MO 65215

1. **Degrees and areas of study:** Bachelor of Arts in the following areas of concentration: business administration, child study, humanities, health science, psychology, social science, and history, as well as individually designed programs; Associate in Arts; Bachelor of Science in Health Information Management

2. **Institutional accreditation:** North Central Association of Colleges and Schools

3. **Previous education required:** Bachelor of Arts and Bachelor of Science, high school diploma or GED equivalent; Bachelor of Science in Health Information Management, certification as an Accredited Record Technician (ART) or Registered Record Administrator (RRA)

4. **Credit for prior learning:** Satisfactory completion of instruction offered by businesses, government agencies, labor unions, or professional or voluntary associations, and evaluated by the American Council on Education; credit upon transfer from other institutions; demonstrated experiential learning (life and occupational experiences); military educational experiences evaluated by the American Council on Education

5. **Credit for successful completion of standardized achievement tests:** College-Level Examination Program (CLEP) General Examinations, College-Level Examination Program (CLEP) Subject Examinations, DANTES Subject Standardized Tests (DSST)

6. **Number of credit hours required for degree:** Bachelor of Arts and Bachelor of Science in Health Information Management, 120 semester hours; Associate in Arts, 60 semester hours

7. **Minimum campus time:** None

8. **Instructional methods provided for off-campus learning:** Correspondence courses, guided instruction via telephone and mail, supervised field work, sponsored experiential learning

9. **Student support services provided:** Academic advising, financial aid, orientation, counseling and testing, career counseling, job placement assistance

10. **Available informational materials:** Student handbook of pertinent policies and procedures, program catalog, program brochure

11. **Grading system:** A, B, C, D, F, or other variation of scale using A, B, C

12. **Enrollment:** Bachelor of Arts, 615; Associate in Arts, none; Bachelor of Science in Health Information Management, 227

13. **Degrees conferred:** Bachelor of Arts, 592; Associate in Arts, 8; Bachelor of Science in Health Information Management, 8

14. **Year begun:** Bachelor of Arts and Associate in Arts, 1972; Bachelor of Science in Health Information Management, 1978

15. **Out-of-state students:** Accepted; tuition same as for in-state students

University of Missouri—Columbia

Health Services Management Program
School of Health Related Professionals
403 Noyes
Columbia, MO 65211

1. **Degrees and areas of study:** Bachelor of Health Science
2. **Institutional accreditation:** North Central Association of Colleges and Schools
3. **Previous education required:** One to two years of college
4. **Credit for prior learning:** Satisfactory completion of instruction offered by businesses, government agencies, labor unions, or professional or voluntary associations, and evaluated by the American Council on Education; credit upon transfer from other institutions; demonstrated experiential learning (life and occupational experiences); military educational experiences evaluated by the American Council on Education
5. **Credit for successful completion of standardized achievement tests:** College-Level Examination Program (CLEP) General Examinations, College-Level Examination Program (CLEP) Subject Examinations, College Board Advanced Placement Examinations
6. **Number of credit hours required for degree:** 120 semester hours
7. **Minimum campus time:** 24 credit hours
8. **Instructional methods provided for off-campus learning:** Correspondence courses, television courses, guided instruction via telephone and mail, packaged course and study guides, cooperative education, supervised field work, sponsored experiential learning
9. **Student support services provided:** Academic advising, orientation, counseling and testing, career counseling, job placement assistance
10. **Available informational materials:** Student handbook of pertinent policies and procedures, program brochure
11. **Grading system:** A, B, C, D, F, or other variation of scale using A, B, C
12. **Enrollment:** 45
13. **Degrees conferred:** 1
14. **Year begun:** 1980
15. **Out-of-state students:** Accepted; tuition same as for in-state students unless enrolled on a full-time basis

University of Missouri—Columbia

Nontraditional Study Program in Agriculture
103D Whitten Hall
Columbia, MO 65211

1. **Degrees and areas of study:** Bachelor of Science in Agriculture
2. **Institutional accreditation:** North Central Association of Colleges and Schools

3. **Previous education required:** High school diploma or GED equivalent

4. **Credit for prior learning:** Satisfactory completion of instruction offered by businesses, government agencies, labor unions, or professional or voluntary associations, and evaluated by the American Council on Education; credit upon transfer from other institutions; demonstrated experiential learning (life and occupational experiences); military educational experiences evaluated by the American Council on Education

5. **Credit for successful completion of standardized achievement tests:** College-Level Examination Program (CLEP) Subject Examinations, College-Level Examination Program (CLEP) General Examinations, American College Testing (ACT) Proficiency Examination Program, College Board Advanced Placement Examinations, DANTES Subject Standardized Tests (DSST)

6. **Number of credit hours required for degree:** 128 semester hours

7. **Minimum campus time:** None

8. **Instructional methods provided for off-campus learning:** Correspondence courses, video cassettes, television courses, guided instruction via telephone and mail, packaged course and study guides, supervised field work, sponsored experiential learning

9. **Student support services provided:** Academic advising, financial aid, orientation, counseling and testing, career counseling, job placement assistance

10. **Available informational materials:** Program brochure

11. **Grading system:** A, B, C, D, F, or other variation of scale using A, B, C

12. **Enrollment:** 130

13. **Degrees conferred:** 22

14. **Year begun:** 1974

15. **Out-of-state students:** Accepted; tuition higher than for in-state students unless six credit hours or less taken per semester

Caldwell College

Ryerson Avenue
Caldwell, NJ 07006

1. **Degrees and areas of study:** Bachelor of Science in business administration; Bachelor of Arts in elementary education, English, history, psychology, religious studies, sociology, and social studies

2. **Institutional accreditation:** Middle States Association of Colleges and Schools

3. **Previous education required:** High school diploma or GED equivalent

4. **Credit for prior learning:** Satisfactory completion of instruction offered by businesses, government agencies, labor unions, or professional or voluntary associations, and evaluated by the American Council on Education; credit upon transfer from other institutions; demonstrated experiential learning (life and occupational experiences); military educational experiences evaluated by the American Council on Education

5. **Credit for successful completion of standardized achievement tests:** College-Level Examination Program (CLEP) Subject Examinations, College-Level Examination Program (CLEP) General Examinations, College Board Advanced Placement Examinations

6. **Number of credit hours required for degree:** 120 semester hours

7. **Minimum campus time:** Students are expected to attend on-campus weekend which is the first weekend (Friday evening and all day Saturday) of each semester. Weekend Program includes orientation, workshops, seminars, and faculty-student interviews

8. **Instructional methods provided for off-campus learning:** Guided instruction via telephone and mail

9. **Student support services provided:** Academic advising, financial aid, orientation, counseling and testing, career counseling, job placement assistance

10. **Available informational materials:** Program brochure

11. **Grading system:** A, B, C, D, F, or other variation of scale using A, B, C

12. **Enrollment:** 120

13. **Degrees conferred:** 24

14. **Year begun:** 1979

15. **Out-of-state students:** Accepted; tuition same as for in-state students

Thomas A. Edison State College

101 West State Street, CN 545
Trenton, NJ 08625

1. **Degrees and areas of study:** Bachelor of Arts, Associate in Arts, Associate in Applied Science in Radiologic Technology, Associate in Science with emphasis in

Management, Bachelor of Science in Business Administration, Bachelor of Science with a concentration in Human Services or Technical Services

2. **Institutional accreditation:** Middle States Association of Colleges and Schools

3. **Previous education required:** None

4. **Credit for prior learning:** Satisfactory completion of instruction offered by businesses, government agencies, labor unions, or professional or voluntary associations, and evaluated by the American Council on Education; credit upon transfer from other institutions; demonstrated experiential learning (life and occupational experiences); military educational experiences evaluated by the American Council on Education

5. **Credit for successful completion of standardized achievement tests:** College-Level Examination Program (CLEP) General Examinations, College-Level Examination Program (CLEP) Subject Examinations, American College Testing (ACT) Proficiency Examination Program, College Board Advanced Placement Examinations, DANTES Subject Standardized Tests (DSST), Thomas Edison College Examination Program (TECEP)

6. **Number of credit hours required for degree:** Bachelor, 120 semester hours; Associate, 60 semester hours

7. **Minimum campus time:** None

8. **Instructional methods provided for off-campus learning:** Edison State College does not provide instruction

9. **Student support services provided:** Academic advising, financial aid, orientation, counseling and testing

10. **Available informational materials:** Student handbook of pertinent policies and procedures, program catalog, program brochure

11. **Grading system:** Transferred work carries letter grades; examinations and individual assessment through portfolio carries credit only

12. **Enrollment:** Bachelor of Arts, 928; Associate in Arts, 679; Associate in Applied Science in Radiologic Technology, 36; Associate in Science with an emphasis in Management, 233; Bachelor of Science in Business Administration, 720; Bachelor of Science with a concentration in Human Services or Technical Services, 635

13. **Degrees conferred:** Bachelor of Arts, 1,275; Associate in Arts, 2,009; Associate in Applied Science in Radiologic Technology, 17; Associate in Science with an emphasis in Management, 111; Bachelor of Science in Business Administration, 219; Bachelor with a concentration in Human Services or Technical Services, 186

14. **Year begun:** Bachelor of Arts, Associate in Applied Science in Radiologic Technology, and Associate in Science with an emphasis in Management, 1974; Associate in Arts and Bachelor of Science in Business Administration, 1972; Bachelor of Science with a concentration in Human Services or Technical Services, 1977

15. **Out-of-state students:** Accepted; tuition higher than for in-state students

College of Santa Fe

School of Open Studies
St. Michaels Drive
Santa Fe, NM 87501

1. **Degrees and areas of study:** Bachelor of Arts
2. **Institutional accreditation:** North Central Association of Colleges and Schools
3. **Previous education required:** High school diploma or GED equivalent
4. **Credit for prior learning:** Satisfactory completion of instruction offered by businesses, government agencies, labor unions, or professional or voluntary associations, and evaluated by the American Council on Education; credit upon transfer from other institutions; demonstrated experiential learning (life and occupational experiences); military educational experiences evaluated by the American Council on Education
5. **Credit for successful completion of standardized achievement tests:** College-Level Examination Program (CLEP) General Examinations, College-Level Examination Program (CLEP) Subject Examinations
6. **Number of credit hours required for degree:** 128 semester hours
7. **Minimum campus time:** An introductory seminar, usually scheduled for three weekends, but also offered one or twice a year in a one-week intensive format
8. **Instructional methods provided for off-campus learning:** Guided instruction via telephone and mail, packaged course and study guides, cooperative education, supervised field work, sponsored experiential learning
9. **Student support services provided:** Academic advising, financial aid, orientation, counseling and testing, career counseling, job placement assistance
10. **Available informational materials:** Student handbook of pertinent policies and procedures, program brochure
11. **Grading system:** A, B, C, D, F, or other variation of scale using A, B, C; a few courses are on a pass/fail basis
12. **Enrollment:** 100
13. **Degrees conferred:** 6
14. **Year begun:** 1980
15. **Out-of-state students:** Accepted; tuition same as for in-state students

Bard College

Independent Studies Program
Annandale-on-Hudson, NY 12504

1. **Degrees and areas of study:** Bachelor of Professional Studies in Human Services; Bachelor of Arts in Independent Studies
2. **Institutional accreditation:** Middle States Association of Colleges and Schools
3. **Previous education required:** Bachelor of Professional Studies in Human Services, one year or less of college; Bachelor of Arts in Independent Studies, one to two years of college
4. **Credit for prior learning:** Satisfactory completion of instruction offered by businesses, government agencies, labor unions, or professional or voluntary associations, and evaluated by the American Council on Education; credit upon transfer from other institutions; demonstrated experiential learning (life and occupational experiences); military educational experiences evaluated by the American Council on Education
5. **Credit for successful completion of standardized achievement tests:** College-Level Examination Program (CLEP) General Examinations, College-Level Examination Program (CLEP) Subject Examinations, DANTES Subject Standardized Tests (DSST)
6. **Number of credit hours required for degree:** 124 semester hours
7. **Minimum campus time:** Campus Day—five hours per semester; tutorials, minimum seven meetings; seminars, 15 two-hour meetings
8. **Instructional methods provided for off-campus learning:** Television courses, guided instruction via telephone and mail, supervised field work, sponsored experiential learning
9. **Student support services provided:** Academic advising, financial aid, orientation
10. **Available informational materials:** Student handbook of pertinent policies and procedures, program brochure
11. **Grading system:** A, B, C, D, F, or other variation of scale using A, B, C
12. **Enrollment:** Bachelor of Professional Studies in Human Services, 20; Bachelor of Arts in Independent Studies, 15
13. **Degrees conferred:** Bachelor of Professional Studies in Human Services, 2; Bachelor of Arts in Independent Studies, 45
14. **Year begun:** Bachelor of Professional Studies in Human Services, 1980; Bachelor of Arts in Independent Studies, 1972
15. **Out-of-state students:** Accepted from contiguous states; tuition same as for in-state students

Empire State College

Saratoga Springs, NY 12866

1. **Degrees and areas of study:** Bachelor of Arts, Bachelor of Science, Bachelor of Professional Studies, Associate of Arts, Associate of Science

2. **Institutional accreditation:** Middle States Association of Colleges and Schools

3. **Previous education required:** High school diploma or GED equivalency

4. **Credit for prior learning:** Satisfactory completion of instruction offered by businesses, government agencies, labor unions, or professional or voluntary associations, and evaluated by the American Council on Education; credit upon transfer from other institutions; demonstrated experiential learning (life and occupational experiences); military educational experiences evaluated by the American Council on Education

5. **Credit for successful completion of standardized achievement tests:** College-Level Examination Program (CLEP) General Examinations, College-Level Examination Program (CLEP) Subject Examinations, American College Testing (ACT) Proficiency Examination Program, College Board Advanced Placement Examinations, DANTES Subject Standardized Tests (DSST), Graduate Record Examinations (GRE)

6. **Number of credit hours required for degree:** Associate, 64 semester hours; Bachelor, 128 semester hours

7. **Minimum campus time:** Associate, none; Bachelor, most students will be expected to complete approximately 32 credits at one of 30 learning centers in New York State

8. **Instructional methods provided for off-campus learning:** Correspondence, television courses, guided instruction via telephone and mail, packaged course and study guides, cooperative education, supervised field work, sponsored experiential learning

9. **Student support services provided:** Academic advising, financial aid, orientation, counseling and testing, job placement assistance

10. **Available informational materials:** Student handbook of pertinent policies and procedures, catalog, brochure

11. **Grading system:** Written evaluation of each learning contract by advisor responsible for the contract

12. **Enrollment:** 3,800

13. **Degrees conferred:** 9,000 (estimated)

14. **Year begun:** 1971

15. **Out-of-state students:** Accepted; tuition higher than for in-state students

Skidmore College

University Without Walls
Saratoga Springs, NY 12866

1. **Degrees and areas of study:** Self-determined major in Bachelor of Arts or Bachelor of Science; students can earn degrees in all areas offered by Skidmore College (69 separate majors)

2. **Institutional accreditation:** Middle States Association of Colleges and Schools

3. **Previous education required:** High school diploma or GED equivalent

4. **Credit for prior learning:** Satisfactory completion of instruction offered by businesses, government agencies, labor unions, or professional or voluntary associations, and evaluated by the American Council on Education; credit upon transfer from other institutions; demonstrated experiential learning (life and occupational experiences); military educational experiences evaluated by the American Council on Education

5. **Credit for successful completion of standardized achievement tests:** College-Level Examination Program (CLEP) General Examinations, College-Level Examination Program (CLEP) Subject Examinations, American College Testing (ACT) Proficiency Examination Program, College Board Advanced Placement Examinations, DANTES Subject Standardized Tests (DSST)

6. **Number of credit hours required for degree:** Individually designed curriculum is expected to contain educational experiences equivalent to those of a traditional Skidmore degree (36 units each worth $3\frac{1}{3}$ credits)

7. **Minimum campus time:** Two separate campus visits for one day each visit: the first one-day session is for advising and preadvising; the second one-day session is for the presentation of the student's degree plan to a committee of the faculty

8. **Instructional methods provided for off-campus learning:** Correspondence courses, guided instruction via telephone and mail, supervised field work, sponsored experiential learning

9. **Student support services provided:** Academic advising, financial aid, orientation, counseling and testing, job placement assistance

10. **Available informational materials:** Program brochure, preadvising packet containing material on all pertinent policies and procedures

11. **Grading system:** There is no predominant grading system; type of evaluation varies according to agreement between student and advisor/mentor/instructor

12. **Enrollment:** 250

13. **Degrees conferred:** 322

14. **Year begun:** 1975

15. **Out-of-state students:** Accepted; tuition same as for in-state students

State University College at Brockport

Division of Public Service/Continuing Education
Brockport, NY 14420

1. **Degrees and areas of study:** Bachelor of Arts in Liberal Arts

2. **Institutional accreditation:** Middle States Association of Colleges and Schools

3. **Previous education required:** High school diploma or GED equivalent

4. **Credit for prior learning:** Satisfactory completion of instruction offered by businesses, government agencies, labor unions, or professional or voluntary associations, and evaluated by the American Council on Education; credit upon transfer from other institutions; demonstrated experiential learning (life and occupational experiences); military educational experiences evaluated by the American Council on Education

5. **Credit for successful completion of standardized achievement tests:** College-Level Examination Program (CLEP) Subject Examinations, College-Level Examination Program (CLEP) General Examinations, College Board Advanced Placement Examinations, American College Testing (ACT) Proficiency Examination Program, DANTES Subject Standardized Tests (DSST)

6. **Number of credit hours required for degree:** 120 semester hours

7. **Minimum campus time:** 24 semester hours

8. **Instructional methods provided for off-campus learning:** Correspondence courses, television courses, packaged course and study guides, cooperative education, supervised field work, sponsored experiential learning

9. **Student support services provided:** Academic advising, orientation, counseling and testing

10. **Available informational materials:** Program catalog, program brochure

11. **Grading system:** A, B, C, D, F, or other variation of scale using A, B, C

12. **Enrollment:** 93

13. **Degrees conferred:** 180 (estimated)

14. **Year begun:** 1971

15. **Out-of-state students:** Accepted; tuition higher than for in-state students

Syracuse University

Independent Study Degree Programs
610 E. Fayette Street
Syracuse, NY 13202

1. **Degrees and areas of study:** Bachelor of Arts in Liberal Studies, Bachelor of Science in Business Administration, Master of Social Science, Master of Business Administration, Master of Fine Arts in Advertising Design, Master of Fine Arts in Illustration

2. **Institutional accreditation:** Middle States Association of Colleges and Schools

3. **Previous education required:** Bachelor degrees, high school diploma or GED equivalent; Master degrees, baccalaureate degree

4. **Credit for prior learning:** Satisfactory completion of instruction offered by businesses, government agencies, labor unions, or professional or voluntary associations, and evaluated by the American Council on Education; credit upon transfer from other institutions; demonstrated experiential learning (life and occupational experiences); military educational experiences evaluated by the American Council on Education

5. **Credit for successful completion of standardized achievement tests:** College-Level Examination Program (CLEP) Subject Examinations, College Board Advanced Placement Examinations, American College Testing (ACT) Proficiency Examination Program, DANTES Subject Standardized Tests (DSST), New York Board of Regents College Proficiency Examination Program (CPEP)

6. **Number of credit hours required for degree:** Bachelor of Arts in Liberal Arts and

Bachelor of Science in Business Administration, 120 semester hours; Master of Social Science, Master of Fine Arts in Advertising Design, and Master of Fine Arts in Illustration, 30 semester hours; Master of Business Administration, 36 52 semester hours

7. **Minimum campus time:** Bachelor programs, one week on campus at the beginning of each semester in which student wishes to study, three semesters per year available; Master of Social Science, two weeks in July for two summers (not necessarily consecutive); Master of Business Administration, one week on campus at the beginning of each semester in which the student wishes to study; Master of Fine Arts in Advertising Design, two weeks on campus for three consecutive years, plus eleven days per year spent meeting in major cities; Master of Fine Arts in Illustration, three two-week seminars in August (consecutive) plus a week in the spring and fall each year in New York City (total two weeks for three summers and eleven days per year for two years)

8. **Instructional methods provided for off-campus learning:** Guided instruction via telephone and mail, supervised field work, sponsored experiential learning, and occasional television courses for bachelor programs only

9. **Student support services provided:** Academic advising, financial aid, orientation, counseling and testing career counseling, job placement assistance

10. **Available informational materials:** External degree program catalog, program brochure, course descriptions; Master of Fine Arts poster describing program in addition to information in catalog

11. **Grading system:** A, B, C, D, F, or other variation of scale using A, B, C

12. **Enrollment:** Bachelor of Arts in Liberal Studies, approximately 300-400; Bachelor of Science in Business Administration, approximately 250; Master of Social Sciences, approximately 200-250; Master of Business Administration, approximately 200; Master of Fine Arts in Advertising Design, approximately 70; Master of Fine Arts in Illustration, approximately 70

13. **Degrees conferred:** 600 700 estimated total for all independent-study degree programs combined

14. **Year begun:** Bachelor of Arts in Liberal Studies, 1966; Bachelor of Science in Business Administration, 1968; Master of Social Science, 1975; Master of Business Administration, 1977; Master of Fine Arts in Advertising Design, 1973; Master of Fine Arts in Illustration, 1973

15. **Out-of-state students:** Accepted; tuition same as for in-state students

University of the State of New York

Regents External Degree Program
Cultural Education Center
Albany, NY 12230

1. **Degrees and areas of study:** Bachelor of Arts, Bachelor of Science, Associate Degree in Arts, Associate Degree in Science, Bachelor of Science in Business, Bachelor of Science in Nursing, Associate in Science in Nursing, Associate in Applied Science in Nursing

2. **Institutional accreditation:** Middle States Association of Colleges and Schools

3. **Previous education required:** None

4. **Credit for prior learning:** Satisfactory completion of instruction offered by businesses, government agencies, labor unions, or professional or voluntary associations, and evaluated by the American Council on Education; credit upon transfer from other institutions; demonstrated experiential learning (life and occupational experiences) (if validated by examination); military educational experiences evaluated by the American Council on Education

5. **Credit for successful completion of standardized achievement tests:** College-Level Examination Program (CLEP) General Examinations, College-Level Examination Program (CLEP) Subject Examinations, American College Testing (ACT) Proficiency Examination Program, College Board Advanced Placement Examinations, DANTES Subject Standardized Tests (DSST), Graduate Record Examinations (GRE) Advanced Tests, New York State College Proficiency Examination Program tests, Regents External Degree program tests

6. **Number of credit hours required for degree:** Bachelor of Arts and Bachelor of Science, 120 semester hours; Associate in Arts and Associate in Science, 60 semester hours; Bachelor of Science in Business, within the General Business Option, 120 semester hours of credit of which 63 are in the general education component and 57 are in the business component. Within the Subject Concentration Option degree requirements are structured in terms of levels of competence in five major business subjects as well as a competence in a general-education component; Bachelor of Science in Nursing, 72 semester hours of general-education credit plus five written and three performance examinations in nursing; Associate in Science in Nursing, 30 semester hours of general education plus seven written and one performance examinations in nursing; Associate in Applied Science in Nursing, 10 one-semester courses or 5 proficiency examinations totaling a minimum of 30 semester hours of general education plus one performance and seven written examinations in nursing

7. **Minimum campus time:** None

8. **Instructional methods provided for off-campus learning:** The Regents External Degree is a noninstructional program

9. **Student support services provided:** Academic advising, financial aid, orientation, career counseling

10. **Available informational materials:** Student handbook of pertinent policies and procedures, program catalog, program brochure, study guides for examinations offered, various information brochures, test applications, *How to Study Independently* brochure, volunteer advisor list

11. **Grading system:** Credits are accepted from approved sources; therefore, grading systems vary

12. **Enrollment:** Bachelor of Arts, 1,507; Bachelor of Science, 5,238; Associate Degree in Arts, 824; Associate Degree in Science, 503; Bachelor of Science in Business, 2,468; Bachelor of Science in Nursing, 4,696; Associate in Science in Nursing, 2,128; Associate in Applied Science in Nursing, 1,318

13. **Degrees conferred:** Bachelor of Arts, 1,443; Bachelor of Science, 4,108; Associate Degree in Arts, 3,893; Associate Degree in Science, 5,449; Bachelor of Science in

Business, 343; Bachelor of Science in Nursing, 281; Associate in Science in Nursing, 784; Associate in Applied Science in Nursing, 454

14. **Year begun:** Bachelor of Arts, Bachelor of Science, and Associate Degree in Science, 1974; Associate Degree in Arts and Bachelor of Science in Business, 1972; Bachelor of Science in Nursing, 1976; Associate in Science in Nursing, 1975; Associate in Applied Science in Nursing, 1973

15. **Out-of-state students:** Accepted; tuition same as for in-state students

Cleveland Institute of Electronics

1776 East 17th Street
Cleveland, OH 44114

1. **Degrees and areas of study:** Associate in Applied Science in Electronics Engineering Technology
2. **Institutional accreditation:** Accrediting Commission of the National Home Study Council
3. **Previous education required:** None
4. **Credit for prior learning:** Credit upon transfer from other institutions; demonstrated experiential learning (life and occupational experiences)
5. **Credit for successful completion of standardized achievement tests:** None
6. **Number of credit hours required for degree:** 106 quarter hours
7. **Minimum campus time:** None
8. **Instructional methods provided for off-campus learning:** Correspondence courses, guided instruction via telephone and mail, packaged course and study guides, library equivalency service (bibliography and borrowing service), instructor mentoring for advanced students to assist in completing program, six-day-per-week tollfree WATS telephone lines
9. **Student support services provided:** Academic advising, financial aid, counseling and testing, job placement assistance
10. **Available informational materials:** Student handbook of pertinent policies and procedures, program catalog, program brochure
11. **Grading system:** Percentage grading, minimum 78 percent grade average to graduate
12. **Enrollment:** 1,500
13. **Degrees conferred:** 11
14. **Year begun:** 1979
15. **Out-of-state students:** Accepted; tuition same as for in-state students

Dyke College

Division of Extended Learning
1375 East 6th Street
Cleveland, OH 44144

1. **Degrees and areas of study:** Bachelor of Science
2. **Institutional accreditation:** North Central Association of Colleges and Schools

3. **Previous education required:** One to two years of college

4. **Credit for prior learning:** Satisfactory completion of instruction offered by businesses, government agencies, labor unions, or professional or voluntary associations, and evaluated by the American Council on Education; credit upon transfer from other institutions; demonstrated experiential learning (life and occupational experiences); military educational experiences evaluated by the American Council on Education

5. **Credit for successful completion of standardized achievement tests:** College-Level Examination Program (CLEP) General Examinations, College-Level Examination Program (CLEP) Subject Examinations, American College Testing (ACT) Proficiency Examination Program, College Board Advanced Placement Examinations, DANTES Subject Standardized Tests (DSST)

6. **Number of credit hours required for degree:** 126 semester hours

7. **Minimum campus time:** None

8. **Instructional methods provided for off-campus learning:** Guided instruction via telephone and mail, cooperative education, supervised field work, sponsored experiential learning

9. **Student support services provided:** Academic advising, financial aid, orientation, counseling and testing, career counseling, job placement assistance

10. **Available informational materials:** Student handbook of pertinent policies and procedures, program catalog, program brochure, guide for documenting requests for life/work experience credits, quarterly newsletter

11. **Grading system:** A, B, C, D, F, or other variation of scale using A, B, C

12. **Enrollment:** 520

13. **Degrees conferred:** 170

14. **Year begun:** 1974

15. **Out-of-state students:** Not accepted

Ohio University

External Student Program
Tupper Hall—Room 301
Athens, OH 45701

1. **Degrees and areas of study:** Associate of Arts, Associate of Science, Associate of Individualized Studies, Associate of Applied Science in Security/Safety Technology, Bachelor of General Studies, Bachelor of Science, Bachelor of Arts, Bachelor of Business Administration

2. **Institutional accreditation:** North Central Association of Colleges and Schools

3. **Previous education required:** High school diploma or GED equivalent

4. **Credit for prior learning:** Credit upon transfer from other institutions; demonstrated experiential learning (life and occupational experiences); military educational experiences evaluated by the American Council on Education

5. **Credit for successful completion of standardized achievement tests:** College-

Level Examination Program (CLEP) Subject Examinations, College Board Advanced Placement Examinations

6. **Number of credit hours required for degree:** Associate of Arts, Associate of Science, Associate of Individualized Studies, Associate of Applied Science in Security/Safety Technology, 96 quarter hours; Bachelor of General Studies, Bachelor of Science, Bachelor of Arts, Bachelor of Business Administration, 192 quarter hours

7. **Minimum campus time:** None

8. **Instructional methods provided for off-campus learning:** Correspondence courses, television courses, packaged course and study guides, sponsored experiential learning

9. **Student support services provided:** Academic advising, career counseling, job placement assistance

10. **Available informational materials:** Student handbook of pertinent policies and procedures, program catalog, program brochure

11. **Grading system:** A, B, C, D, F, or other variation of scale using A, B, C

12. **Enrollment:** Associate of Arts, 40; Associate of Science, 6; Associate of Individualized Studies, 39; Associate of Applied Science in Security/Safety Technology, 40; Bachelor of General Studies, 350; Bachelor of Science, Bachelor of Arts, and Bachelor of Business Administration, 100

13. **Degrees conferred:** Associate of Arts, 6; Associate of Science, Associate of Individualized Studies, Associate of Applied Science in Security/Safety Technology, none; Bachelor of General Studies, 19; Bachelor of Science, Bachelor of Arts, Bachelor of Business Administration, none

14. **Year begun:** Associate of Arts, Associate of Individualized Studies, Bachelor of General Studies, Bachelor of Science, Bachelor of Arts, Bachelor of Business Administration, 1974; Associate of Science, 1981; Associate of Applied Science in Security/Safety Technology, 1980

15. **Out-of-state students:** Accepted; tuition same as for in-state students

University of Cincinnati

Division of Graduate Education and Research
Cincinnati, OH 45221

1. **Degrees and areas of study:** Master of Science in Community Health Planning/Administration

2. **Institutional accreditation:** North Central Association of Colleges and Secondary Schools

3. **Previous education required:** Baccalaureate degree

4. **Credit for prior learning:** Credit upon transfer from other institutions

5. **Credit for successful completion of standardized achievement tests:** None

6. **Number of credit hours required for degree:** 60 quarter hours

7. **Minimum campus time:** Two-day orientation in September prior to beginning

study and a two-day seminar meeting once per academic quarter excluding summer quarter; meeting sites in Cincinnati, Columbus, and Cleveland, Ohio, and Nashville, Tennessee

8. **Instructional methods provided for off-campus learning:** Guided instruction via telephone and mail, packaged course and study guides, sponsored experiential learning

9. **Student support services provided:** Academic advising, orientation, counseling and testing, career counseling, job placement assistance

10. **Available informational materials:** Student handbook of pertinent policies and procedures, program brochure

11. **Grading system:** A, B, C, D, F, or other variation of scale using A, B, C

12. **Enrollment:** 165

13. **Degrees conferred:** 60 (estimated)

14. **Year begun:** 1975

15. **Out-of-state students:** Accepted; tuition higher than for in-state students

Ursuline College

Center for Continuing Studies
2550 Lander Road
Pepper Pike, OH 44124

1. **Degrees and areas of study:** Bachelor of Arts

2. **Institutional accreditation:** North Central Association of Colleges and Schools

3. **Previous education required:** High school diploma or GED equivalent and 45 semester (68 quarter) hours

4. **Credit for prior learning:** Satisfactory completion of instruction offered by businesses, government agencies, labor unions, or professional or voluntary associations, and evaluated by the American Council on Education; credit upon transfer from other institutions; demonstrated experiential learning (life and occupational experiences); military educational experiences evaluated by the American Council on Education

5. **Credit for successful completion of standardized achievement tests:** College-Level Examination Program (CLEP) Subject Examinations, College-Level Examination Program (CLEP) General Examinations

6. **Number of credit hours required for degree:** 128 semester hours

7. **Minimum campus time:** Four-hour orientation session, plus four on-campus student-faculty discussion sessions for each project pursued independently

8. **Instructional methods provided for off-campus learning:** Packaged course and study guides, supervised field work

9. **Student support services provided:** Academic advising, financial aid, orientation, counseling and testing, career counseling, job placement assistance

10. **Available informational materials:** Student handbook of pertinent policies and

procedures, program catalog, program brochure, guide for the preparation of life experience

11. **Grading system:** A, B, C, D, F, or other variation of scale using A, B, C

12. **Enrollment:** 105

13. **Degrees conferred:** 120

14. **Year begun:** 1975

15. **Out-of-state students:** Not accepted

Oklahoma City University

Competency-Based Degree Program
2501 North Blackwelder
Oklahoma City, OK 73106

1. **Degrees and areas of study:** Bachelor of Arts or Bachelor of Science Degree
2. **Institutional accreditation:** North Central Association of Colleges and Schools
3. **Previous education required:** High school diploma or GED equivalent
4. **Credit for prior learning:** Satisfactory completion of instruction offered by businesses, government agencies, labor unions, or professional or voluntary associations, and evaluated by the American Council on Education; credit upon transfer from other institutions; demonstrated experiential learning (life and occupational experiences); military educational experiences evaluated by the American Council on Education
5. **Credit for successful completion of standardized achievement tests:** College-Level Examination Program (CLEP) General Examinations, College-Level Examination Program (CLEP) Subject Examinations, American College Testing (ACT) Proficiency Examination Program, College Board Advanced Placement Examinations, DANTES Subject Standardized Tests (DSST), College General Education Development (GED) Examinations, Graduate Record Examination (GRE) Advanced Tests, Certified Professional Secretary (CPS) Test. The following licenses and certificates are also recognized: Certified Public Accountant (CPA), Chartered Life Underwriter (CLU), Chartered Property, Casualty Underwriter (CPCU), Federal Communications Commission (FCC) License, First/Second Class Aviation Licenses
6. **Number of credit hours required for degree:** 124 semester hours
7. **Minimum campus time:** Students must meet occasionally with faculty as requested and attend a 1-day initial orientation session
8. **Instructional methods provided for off-campus learning:** Correspondence courses, video cassettes, television courses, guided instruction via telephone and mail, packaged course and study guides, supervised field work, sponsored experiential learning
9. **Student support services provided:** Academic advising, financial aid, orientation, counseling and testing, career counseling, job placement assistance
10. **Available informational materials:** Student handbook of pertinent policies and procedures, program catalog, program brochure
11. **Grading system:** A, B, C, D, F, or other variation of scale using A, B, C
12. **Enrollment:** 204
13. **Degrees conferred:** 150

14. **Year begun:** 1974
15. **Out-of-state students:** Accepted; tuition same as for in-state students

University of Oklahoma

College of Liberal Studies
1700 Asp Avenue
Norman, OK 73037

1. **Degrees and areas of study:** Bachelor of Liberal Studies (BLS), Bachelor of Liberal Studies—Upper Division Option (BLS-UDO), Master of Liberal Studies (MLS)
2. **Institutional accreditation:** North Central Association of Colleges and Secondary Schools
3. **Previous education required:** BLS, high school diploma or GED equivalent, BLS-UDO, Associate degree from an accredited institution or minimum of 60 semester hours transferable to the University of Oklahoma; MLS, regular admission: minimum of 3.0 on 4.0 scale; provisional admission: minimum of 2.75 on 4.0 scale
4. **Credit for prior learning:** Bachelor's degrees, credit upon transfer from other institutions, military educational experiences evaluated by the American Council on Education; Master's degrees, none
5. **Credit for successful completion of standardized achievement tests:** Bachelor's, College-Level Examination Program (CLEP) Subject Examinations, College Board Advanced Placement Examinations, American College Testing (ACT) Proficiency Examination Program, DANTES Subject Standardized Tests (DSST); Master's, none
6. **Number of credit hours required for degree:** BLS, 124 semester hours; BLS-UDO, 65 semester hours; MLS, 32 semester hours
7. **Minimum campus time:** Bachelor's, three area seminars in humanities, natural sciences, and sessions in January and June; Master's, introductory one-week seminar at beginning, a three-week MLS Colloquium at midpoint, and a three-week advanced seminar at the end of the program
8. **Instructional methods provided for off-campus learning:** Bachelor's, guided instruction via telephone and mail, packaged course and study guides, supervised field work, sponsored experiential learning; Master's, guided instruction via telephone and mail, supervised field work, sponsored experiential learning
9. **Student support services provided:** Academic advising, financial aid, orientation, counseling and testing, job placement assistance, career counseling
10. **Available informational materials:** Bachelor's, student handbook of pertinent policies and procedures, program catalog, program brochure; quarterly newsletter and all required books are furnished on a loan basis; Master's, student handbook of pertinent policies and procedures, program catalog, program brochure

11. **Grading system:** Bachelor's, scores are "pass," "pass with deficiency" (faculty advisor assigns additional work), and "restudy-retest" (after more study, the student tries another form of the test). Only a passing score is recorded as "S"; Master's, successful completion of work is awarded "S" for that particular MLS phase; students who do not meet expectations withdraw or are withdrawn

12. **Enrollment:** BLS, 247; BLS-UDO, 288; MLS, 150

13. **Degrees conferred:** BLS, 685; BLS-UDO, 75; MLS, 132

14. **Year begun:** BLS, 1961; BLS-UDO, 1972; MLS, 1968

15. **Out-of-state students:** Accepted; tuition higher than for in-state students

Eastern Oregon State College

External Degree Program
La Grande, OR 97850

1. **Degrees and areas of study:** Bachelor of Science in General Studies
2. **Institutional accreditation:** Northwest Association of Schools and Colleges
3. **Previous education required:** High school diploma or GED equivalent
4. **Credit for prior learning:** Satisfactory completion of instruction offered by businesses, government agencies, labor unions, or professional or voluntary associations, and evaluated by the American Council on Education; credit upon transfer from other institutions; demonstrated experiential learning (life and occupational experiences); military educational experiences evaluated by the American Council on Education
5. **Credit for successful completion of standardized achievement tests:** College-Level Examination Program (CLEP) General Examinations, College-Level Examination Program (CLEP) Subject Examinations, American College Testing (ACT) Proficiency Examination Program
6. **Number of credit hours required for degree:** 186 quarter hours
7. **Minimum campus time:** None
8. **Instructional methods provided for off-campus learning:** Correspondence courses, video cassettes, television courses, guided instruction via telephone and mail, packaged course and study guides, cooperative education, supervised field work
9. **Student support services provided:** Academic advising, financial aid, orientation, counseling and testing, career counseling, job placement assistance
10. **Available informational materials:** Student handbook of pertinent policies and procedures, program catalog, program brochure
11. **Grading system:** Credit/no credit
12. **Enrollment:** Approximately 200
13. **Degrees conferred:** 20 (estimated)
14. **Year begun:** 1979
15. **Out-of-state students:** Accepted; tuition same as for in-state students

Linfield College

McMinnville, OR 97128

1. **Degrees and areas of study:** Bachelor of Science in Management; Bachelor of Arts in Liberal Studies

2. **Institutional accreditation:** Northwest Association of Schools and Colleges

3. **Previous education required:** High school diploma or GED equivalency

4. **Credit for prior learning:** Satisfactory completion of instruction offered by businesses, government agencies, labor unions, or professional or voluntary associations, and evaluated by the American Council on Education; credit upon transfer from other institutions; demonstrated experiential learning (life and occupational experiences); military educational experiences evaluated by the American Council on Education

5. **Credit for successful completion of standardized achievement tests:** College-Level Examination Program (CLEP) General Examinations, College-Level Examination Program (CLEP) Subject Examinations, College Board Advanced Placement Examinations, American College Testing (ACT) Proficiency Examination Program

6. **Number of credit hours required for degree:** 125

7. **Minimum campus time:** 30 semester hours must be taken at off-campus locations through the state

8. **Instructional methods provided for off-campus learning:** Correspondence courses, video cassettes, television courses, guided instruction via telephone and mail, supervised field work

9. **Student support services provided:** Academic advising, financial aid, orientation, counseling and testing

10. **Available informational materials:** Student handbook of pertinent policies and procedures, program catalog, program brochure

11. **Grading system:** A, B, C, D, F, or other variation of scale using A, B, C

12. **Enrollment:** Bachelor of Science in Management, 179; Bachelor of Arts in Liberal Studies, 260

13. **Degrees conferred:** Bachelor of Science in Management, 3; Bachelor of Arts in Liberal Studies, 300 (estimated)

14. **Year begun:** Bachelor of Science in Management, 1981; Bachelor of Arts in Liberal Studies, 1975

15. **Out-of-state students:** Accepted on a limited, special-arrangement basis; tuition same as for in-state students

Marylhurst College for Lifelong Learning

Individualized Degree Program
Marylhurst, OR 97034

1. **Degrees and areas of study:** Bachelor of Arts in interdisciplinary studies, communications, humanities/social science, and science/math

2. **Institutional accreditation:** Northwest Association of Schools and Colleges

3. **Previous education required:** High school diploma or GED equivalency

4. **Credit for prior learning:** Satisfactory completion of instruction offered by businesses, government agencies, labor unions, or professional or voluntary

associations, and evaluated by the American Council on Education; credit upon transfer from other institutions; demonstrated experiential learning (life and occupational experiences); military educational experiences evaluated by the American Council on Education

5. **Credit for successful completion of standardized achievement tests:** College-Level Examination Program (CLEP) General Examinations, College-Level Examination Program (CLEP) Subject Examinations, American College Testing (ACT) Proficiency Examination Program

6. **Number of credit hours required for degree:** 180 quarter hours

7. **Minimum campus time:** 20 quarter hours

8. **Instructional methods provided for off-campus learning:** Correspondence courses, video cassettes, television courses, newspaper courses, guided instruction via telephone and mail, computer-assisted, self-paced instruction, packaged course and study guides, cooperative education, supervised field work, sponsored experiential learning

9. **Student support services provided:** Academic advising, financial aid, orientation, counseling and testing, job placement assistance, career counseling

10. **Available informational materials:** Student handbook of pertinent policies and procedures, program catalog, program brochure

11. **Grading system:** A, B, C, D, F, or other variation of scale using A, B, C

12. **Enrollment:** 330

13. **Degrees conferred:** 261

14. **Year begun:** 1976

15. **Out-of-state students:** Accepted; tuition same as for in-state students

Western Oregon State College

Division of Liberal Arts and Sciences
Monmouth, OR 97361

1. **Degrees and areas of study:** Bachelor of Arts or Bachelor of Science in interdisciplinary Studies

2. **Institutional accreditation:** Northwest Association of Schools and Colleges

3. **Previous education required:** High school diploma or GED equivalent

4. **Credit for prior learning:** Credit upon transfer from other institutions

5. **Credit for successful completion of standardized achievement tests:** College-Level Examination Program (CLEP) Subject Examinations, College Board Advanced Placement Examinations

6. **Number of credit hours required for degree:** 192 quarter hours

7. **Minimum campus time:** None

8. **Instructional methods provided for off-campus learning:** Correspondence courses, video cassettes

9. **Student support services provided:** Academic advising, financial aid, orientation, counseling and testing career counseling

10. **Available informational materials:** Program brochure
11. **Grading system:** A, B, C, D, F, or other variation of scale using A, B, C
12. **Enrollment:** None
13. **Degrees conferred:** None
14. **Year begun:** 1982
15. **Out-of-state students:** Accepted; tuition same as for in-state students

Elizabethtown College

Adult External Degree Program
Elizabethtown, PA 17022

1. **Degrees and areas of study:** Bachelor of Professional Studies
2. **Institutional accreditation:** Middle States Association of Schools and Colleges
3. **Previous education required:** 50 semester hours of credit from an accredited institution
4. **Credit for prior learning:** Satisfactory completion of instruction offered by businesses, government agencies, labor unions, or professional or voluntary associations, and evaluated by the American Council on Education; credit upon transfer from other institutions; demonstrated experiential learning (life and occupational experiences); military educational experiences evaluated by the American Council on Education
5. **Credit for successful completion of standardized achievement tests:** College-Level Examination Program (CLEP) General Examinations, College-Level Examination Program (CLEP) Subject Examinations, American College Testing (ACT) Proficiency Examination Program, College Board Advanced Placement Examinations, DANTES Subject Standardized Tests (DSST)
6. **Number of credit hours required for degree:** 128 semester hours
7. **Minimum campus time:** Initial conference with faculty advisor, three one-day-long sessions of a humanities seminar
8. **Instructional methods provided for off-campus learning:** Guided instruction via telephone and mail
9. **Student support services provided:** Academic advising, financial aid, counseling and testing, career counseling, job placement assistance
10. **Available informational materials:** Program brochure, periodic bulletins with information on pertinent policies and procedures
11. **Grading system:** Pass/fail, credit/no credit, or other variation of this scale
12. **Enrollment:** 131
13. **Degrees conferred:** 300 (estimated)
14. **Year begun:** 1972
15. **Out-of-state students:** Accepted; tuition same as for in-state students

Gannon University

The Open University Program—Erie
Metropolitan College of Gannon University
7th and Peach Streets
Erie, PA 16541

1. **Degrees and areas of study:** Associate in Liberal Arts, Associate in Business Administration

2. **Institutional accreditation:** Middle States Association of Colleges and Schools

3. **Previous education required:** High school diploma or GED equivalency

4. **Credit for prior learning:** Satisfactory completion of instruction offered by businesses, government agencies, labor unions, or professional or voluntary associations, and evaluated by the American Council on Education; credit upon transfer from other institutions; military educational experiences evaluated by the American Council on Education

5. **Credit for successful completion of standardized achievement tests:** College-Level Examination Program (CLEP) General Examinations, College-Level Examination Program (CLEP) Subject Examinations, College Board Advanced Placement Examinations

6. **Number of credit hours required for degree:** 66 semester hours

7. **Minimum campus time:** None

8. **Instructional methods provided for off-campus learning:** Correspondence courses, video cassettes, television courses, packaged course and study guides

9. **Student support services provided:** Academic advising, financial aid, orientation, counseling and testing, job placement assistance

10. **Available informational materials:** Student handbook of pertinent policies and procedures, program catalog, program brochure

11. **Grading system:** A, B, C, D, F, or other variation of scale using A, B, C

12. **Enrollment:** 94

13. **Degrees conferred:** None

14. **Year begun:** 1980

15. **Out-of-state students:** Accepted; tuition same as for in-state students

ICS (International Correspondence Schools) Center for Degree Studies

Scranton, PA 18515

1. **Degrees and areas of study:** Associate in Specialized Business in Accounting, Business Management; Associate in Specialized Technology in Civil Engineering Technology, Electrical Engineering Technology, Electronics Technology, Mechanical Drafting and Design Technology, Mechanical Engineering Technology

2. **Institutional accreditation:** Middle States Association of Colleges and Schools

3. **Previous education required:** High school diploma or GED equivalency

4. **Credit for prior learning:** Credit upon transfer from other institutions; demonstrated experiential learning (life and occupational experiences); military educational experiences evaluated by the American Council on Education

5. **Credit for successful completion of standardized achievement tests:** College-Level Examination Program (CLEP) General Examinations, College-Level Examination Program (CLEP) Subject Examinations, American College Testing (ACT) Proficiency Examination Program, DANTES Subject Standardized Tests (DSST)

6. **Number of credit hours required for degree:** Associate in Specialized Business in Accounting and Business Management, 60 semester hours; Associate in Specialized

Technology in Civil Engineering Technology and Electrical Engineering Technology, 66 semester hours; Electronics Technology, 67 semester hours; Mechanical Drafting and Design Technology, 61 semester hours; Mechanical Engineering Technology, 64 semester hours

7. **Minimum campus time:** Associate in Specialized Business in Accounting, Business Management, none; Associate in Specialized Technology in Civil Engineering Technology, Electrical Engineering Technology, Electronics Technology, Mechanical Drafting and Design Technology, and Mechanical Engineering Technology, two-week resident laboratory

8. **Instructional methods provided for off-campus learning:** Correspondence courses, guided instruction via telephone and mail, packaged course and study guides

9. **Student support services provided:** Academic advising, counseling and testing, career counseling

10. **Available informational materials:** Student handbook of pertinent policies and procedures, program catalog

11. **Grading system:** A, B, C, D, F, or other variation of scale using A, B, C

12. **Enrollment:** Associate in Specialized Business in Accounting, 2,880; Business Management, 2,960; Associate in Specialized Technology in Civil Engineering Technology, 800; Electrical Engineering Technology, 400; Electronics Technology, 400; Mechanical Drafting and Design Technology, 80; Mechanical Engineering Technology, 600

13. **Degrees conferred:** Associate in Specialized Business in Accounting, 45; Business Management, 128; Associate in Specialized Technology in Civil Engineering Technology, 35; Electrical Engineering Technology, 36; Electronics Technology, 2; Mechanical Drafting and Design Technology, 3; Mechanical Engineering Technology, 48

14. **Year begun:** Associate in Specialized Business in Accounting, Business Management, Associate in Specialized Technology in Civil Engineering Technology, Electrical Engineering Technology and Mechanical Engineering Technology, 1975; Associate in Specialized Technology in Electronics Technology, Mechanical Drafting and Design Technology, 1977

15. **Out-of-state students:** Accepted; tuition same as for in-state students

Marywood College

Off-Campus Degree Programs
Scranton, PA 18509

1. **Degrees and areas of study:** Bachelor of Science in Business Administration, Bachelor of Science in Accounting

2. **Institutional accreditation:** Middle States Association of Colleges and Schools

3. **Previous education required:** High school diploma or GED equivalent

4. **Credit for prior learning:** Satisfactory completion of instruction offered by businesses, government agencies, labor unions, or professional or voluntary associations, and evaluated by the American Council on Education; credit upon

transfer from other institutions; demonstrated experiential learning (life and. occupational experiences); military educational experiences evaluated by the American Council on Education

5. **Credit for successful completion of standardized achievement tests:** College-Level Examination Program (CLEP) General Examinations, College Board Advanced Placement Examinations, American College Testing (ACT) Proficiency Examination Program, DANTES Subject Standardized Tests (DSST)

6. **Number of credit hours required for degree:** 126 semester hours

7. **Minimum campus time:** Two residencies, each two weeks long; residencies are offered in spring, summer, and fall

8. **Instructional methods provided for off-campus learning:** Correspondence courses, guided instruction via telephone and mail, packaged course and study guides

9. **Student support services provided:** Academic advising, orientation, counseling and testing

10. **Available informational materials:** Program brochure, financial facts, time limits policies, portfolio assessment materials

11. **Grading system:** A, B, C, D, F, or other variation of scale using A, B, C

12. **Enrollment:** 500

13. **Degrees conferred:** 105

14. **Year begun:** 1975

15. **Out-of-state students:** Accepted; tuition same as for in-state students

Pennsylvania State University

College of the Liberal Arts for Letters, Arts, and Sciences or
College of Human Development for Hotel and Food Service
University Park, PA 16802

1. **Degrees and areas of study:** Associate Degree in Letters, Arts, and Sciences; Associate of Science in Hotel and Food Service (emphasis in Health Facility Food Service Administration

2. **Institutional accreditation:** Middle States Association of Colleges and Schools

3. **Previous education required:** High school diploma or GED equivalent

4. **Credit for prior learning:** Associate Degree in Letters, Arts, and Sciences, credit upon transfer from other institutions; demonstrated experiential learning (life and occupational experiences); military educational experiences evaluated by the American Council on Education. Associate of Science, credit upon transfer from other institutions; military educational experiences evaluated by the American Council on Education

5. **Credit for successful completion of standardized achievement tests:** Associate Degree in Letters, Arts, and Sciences, College-Level Examination Program (CLEP) General Examinations, College-Level Examination Program (CLEP) Subject Examinations, American College Testing (ACT) Proficiency Examination Program, College Board Advanced Placement Examinations, DANTES Subject

Standardized Tests (DSST); Associate of Science, College-Level Examination Program (CLEP) Subject Examinations

6. **Number of credit hours required for degree:** Associate Degree in Letters, Arts, and Sciences, 60 semester hours; Associate of Science, 68 semester hours

7. **Minimum campus time:** None

8. **Instructional methods provided for off-campus learning:** Associate Degree in Letters, Arts, and Sciences, correspondence courses, television courses, supervised field work; Associate of Science, correspondence courses, television courses, guided instruction via telephone and mail, packaged course and study guides, supervised field work

9. **Student support services provided:** Associate Degree in Letters, Arts, and Sciences, academic advising, financial aid, orientation, counseling and testing, career counseling, job placement assistance; Associate of Science, academic advising, orientation, counseling and testing, career counseling, job placement assistance

10. **Available informational materials:** Associate in Letters, Arts, and Sciences, student handbook of pertinent policies and procedures, program catalog, program brochure; Associate of Science, student handbook of pertinent policies and procedures, program brochure, independent study by correspondence catalog, Penn. State Bulletin for Associate Degree Programs, program newsletter

11. **Grading system:** A, B, C, D, F, or other variation of scale using A, B, C

12. **Enrollment:** Associate Degree in Letters, Arts, and Sciences, 103; Associate of Science, 118

13. **Degrees conferred:** Associate Degree in Letters, Arts, and Sciences, 750; Associate of Science, none

14. **Year begun:** Associate Degree in Letters, Arts, and Sciences, 1973; Associate of Science, 1977

15. **Out-of-state students:** Associate Degree in Letters, Arts, and Sciences, accepted, tuition higher than for in-state students; Associate of Science, accepted, tuition same as for in-state students

University of Pittsburgh

University External Studies Program
3808 Forbes Avenue
Pittsburgh, PA 15260

1. **Degrees and areas of study:** Bachelor of Arts or Bachelor of Science. External course offerings include all courses needed to fulfill the general degree requirements in the College of General Studies as well as those courses required for a degree in economics, public administration, psychology, or for a social science concentration or a self-designed major. For all other majors offered by the College of General Studies, a student can earn between 75 and 90 of the 120 credits needed for graduation

2. **Institutional accreditation:** Middle States Association of Colleges and Schools

3. **Previous education required:** High school diploma or GED equivalent

4. **Credit for prior learning:** Credit upon transfer from other institutions

5. **Credit for successful completion of standardized achievement tests:** College-Level Examination Program (CLEP) General Examinations, DANTES Subject Standardized Tests (DSST)

6. **Number of credit hours required for degree:** 120 semester hours

7. **Minimum campus time:** Each three-credit course has three, three-hour classes called "workshops" that meet on Saturdays during the term. While "workshops" are an important part of each course, they are mandatory for only two courses. The university operates on a trimester system with terms starting in September, January, and May

8. **Instructional methods provided for off-campus learning:** Guided instruction via telephone and mail, packaged course and study guides

9. **Student support services provided:** Academic advising, financial aid, orientation, counseling and testing, career counseling, job placement assistance

10. **Available informational materials:** Student handbook of pertinent policies and procedures, program catalog, program brochure

11. **Grading system:** A, B, C, D, F, or other variation of scale using A, B, C; however, by special requisition a student may request another form of grading

12. **Enrollment:** Approximately 1,200 per term

13. **Degrees conferred:** Cannot be estimated

14. **Year begun:** 1972

15. **Out-of-state students:** Accepted; tuition higher than for in-state students

RHODE ISLAND

Roger Williams College

The Open Division
Bristol, RI 02809

1. **Degrees and areas of study:** Bachelor of Arts in Humanities, Bachelor of Arts in Fine Arts, Bachelor or Urban and Environmental Planning, Bachelor of Arts in Historic Preservation, Bachelor of Arts in Career Writing and Communication, Bachelor of Science in Computer Science, Bachelor of Science in Civil Engineering Technology, Bachelor of Science in Electrical Engineering Technology, Bachelor of Science in Mechanical Engineering Technology, Bachelor of Science in Electronics Technology, Bachelor of Science in Architectural Technology, Bachelor of Science in Construction Science, Bachelor of Science in Criminal Justice, Bachelor of Science in Industrial Technology, Bachelor of Science in Business Administration, Bachelor of Science in Social and Health Services, Bachelor of Science in Public Administration, Bachelor of Arts in Social Science, Bachelor of Arts in Psychology, Associate of Science in Early Childhood Education

2. **Institutional accreditation:** New England Association of Schools and Colleges

3. **Previous education required:** High school diploma or GED equivalent

4. **Credit for prior learning:** Satisfactory completion of instruction offered by businesses, government agencies, labor unions, or professional or voluntary associations, and evaluated by the American Council on Education; credit upon transfer from other institutions; demonstrated experiential learning (life and occupational experiences); military educational experiences evaluated by the American Council on Education

5. **Credit for successful completion of standardized achievement tests:** College-Level Examination Program (CLEP) General Examinations, College-Level Examination Program (CLEP) Subject Examinations, American College Testing (ACT) Proficiency Examination Program, DANTES Subject Standardized Tests (DSST)

6. **Number of credit hours required for degree:** Bachelor, 40 units (equal to 40 three-credit courses; associate, 20 units (equal to 20 three-credit courses)

7. **Minimum campus time:** None

8. **Instructional methods provided for off-campus learning:** Bachelor of Arts in Humanities, correspondence courses, television courses, newspaper courses, guided instruction via telephone and mail, computer-assisted, self-paced instruction, packaged course and study guides; Bachelor of Arts in Fine Arts, correspondence courses, newspaper courses, guided instruction via telephone and mail, cooperative education, supervised field work; Bachelor of Arts in Historic Preservation and Bachelor of Arts in Career Writing and Communication, correspondence courses, guided instruction via telephone and mail, packaged course and study

guides, cooperative education, supervised field work; Bachelor of Arts in Historic Preservation, correspondence courses, guided instruction via telephone and mail, cooperative education, supervised field work; Bachelor of Science in Computer Science, Bachelor of Science in Civil Engineering Technology, Bachelor of Science in Electrical Engineering Technology, Bachelor of Science in Mechanical Engineering Technology, Bachelor of Science in Electronics Technology, Bachelor of Science in Architectural Technology, Bachelor of Science in Construction Science, Bachelor of Science in Criminial Justice, Bachelor of Science in Industrial Technology, Bachelor of Science in Business Administration, Bachelor of Science in Social and Health Services, Bachelor of Science in Public Administration, Bachelor of Arts in Social Science, Bachelor of Arts in Psychology, correspondence courses, guided instruction via telephone and mail, and supervised field work; Associate of Science in Early Childhood Education, correspondence courses, guided instruction via telephone and mail, cooperative education, supervised field work

9. **Student support services provided:** Academic advising, financial aid, orientation, counseling and testing, career counseling, job placement assistance

10. **Available informational materials:** Student handbook of pertinent policies and procedures, program catalog, program brochure

11. **Grading system:** A, B, C, D, F, or other variation of scale using A, B, C

12. **Enrollment:** Bachelor of Arts in Humanities, 6; Bachelor of Arts in Fine Arts, 8; Bachelor of Urban and Environmental Planning, 6; Bachelor of Arts in Historic Preservation, 8; Bachelor of Arts in Career Writing and Communication, 5; Bachelor of Science in Computer Science, 56; Bachelor of Science in Civil Engineering Technology, 8; Bachelor of Science in Electrical Engineering Technology, 8; Bachelor of Science in Mechanical Engineering Technology, 15; Bachelor of Science in Electronics Technology, 12; Bachelor of Science in Architectural Technology, 10; Bachelor of Science in Construction Science, 10; Bachelor of Science in Criminal Justice, 60; Bachelor of Science in Industrial Technology, 84; Bachelor of Science in Business Administration, 36; Bachelor of Science in Social and Health Services, 78; Bachelor of Science in Public Administration, 55; Bachelor of Arts in Social Science, 14; Bachelor of Arts in Psychology, 16; Associate of Science in Early Childhood Education, 6

13. **Degrees conferred:** Bachelor of Arts in Humanities, 7; Bachelor of Arts in Fine Arts, 24; Bachelor of Science in Urban and Environmental Planning, 4; Bachelor of Arts in Historic Preservation, 5; Bachelor of Arts in Career Writing and Communication, 3; Bachelor of Science in Computer Science, 8; Bachelor of Science in Civil Engineering Technology, 8; Bachelor of Science in Electrical Engineering Technology, 16; Bachelor of Science in Mechanical Engineering Technology, 3; Bachelor of Science in Electronics Technology, 8; Bachelor of Science in Architectural Technology, 8; Bachelor of Science in Construction Science, 6; Bachelor of Science in Criminal Justice, 66; Bachelor of Science in Industrial Technology, 38; Bachelor of Science in Business Administration, 69; Bachelor of Science in Social and Health Services, 246; Bachelor of Science in Public Administration, 41; Bachelor of Arts in Social Science, 24; Bachelor of Arts in Psychology, 26; Associate of Science in Early Childhood Education, 5

14. **Year begun:** Bachelor of Arts in Humanities, Bachelor of Arts in Fine Arts,

Bachelor of Science in Mechanical Engineering Technology, Bachelor of Science in Architectural Technology, Bachelor of Science in Criminal Justice, Bachelor of Science in Industrial Technology, Bachelor of Science in Business Administration, Bachelor of Science in Social and Health Services, Bachelor of Arts in Public Administration, Bachelor of Arts in Social Science, Bachelor of Arts in Psychology, 1974; Bachelor of Science in Urban and Environmental Planning, Bachelor of Arts in Career Writing and Communication, Associate of Science in Early Childhood Education, 1980; Bachelor of Arts in Historic Preservation, 1978; Bachelor of Science in Computer Science, 1979; Bachelor of Science in Civil Engineering Technology, Bachelor of Science in Electrical Engineering Technology, 1975; Bachelor of Science in Electronics Technology, 1976; Bachelor of Science in Construction Science, 1982

15. **Out-of-state students:** Accepted; tuition same as for in-state students

Memphis State University

University College
Memphis, TN 38152

1. **Degrees and areas of study:** Bachelor of Liberal Studies
2. **Institutional accreditation:** Southern Association of Colleges and Schools
3. **Previous education required:** High school diploma or GED equivalent
4. **Credit for prior learning:** Satisfactory completion of instruction offered by businesses, government agencies, labor unions, or professional or voluntary associations, and evaluated by the American Council on Education; credit upon transfer from other institutions; demonstrated experiential learning (life and occupational experiences); military educational experiences evaluated by the American Council on Education
5. **Credit for successful completion of standardized achievement tests:** College-Level Examination Program (CLEP) Subject Examinations, College Board Advanced Placement Examinations, American College Testing (ACT) Proficiency Examination Program (if listed on transcript from another college), DANTES Subject Standardized Tests (DSST) (selected courses)
6. **Number of credit hours required for degree:** 132 semester hours
7. **Minimum campus time:** None
8. **Instructional methods provided for off-campus learning:** Video cassettes, television courses, guided instruction via telephone and mail, packaged course and study guides, supervised field work, sponsored experiential learning
9. **Student support services provided:** Academic advising, financial aid, orientation, counseling and testing, career counseling, job placement assistance
10. **Available informational materials:** Student handbook of pertinent policies and procedures and program brochure
11. **Grading system:** A, B, C, D, F, or other variation of scale using A, B, C
12. **Enrollment:** None (data collected before program began)
13. **Degrees conferred:** None
14. **Year begun:** 1982
15. **Out-of-state students:** Accepted; tuition is $2 per credit hour higher than for in-state students

Brigham Young University

Department of Independent Study
206 Harmon Continuing Education Building
Provo, UT 84602

1. **Degrees and areas of study:** Associate of Science in Home and Family Development, Associate of Arts in Family and Local History Studies, Associate of Science in Justice Administration

2. **Institutional accreditation:** Northwest Association of Schools and Colleges

3. **Previous education required:** High school diploma or GED equivalency

4. **Credit for prior learning:** Associate of Science in Home and Family Development and Associate of Arts in Family and Local History Studies, credit upon transfer from other institutions, military educational experiences evaluated by the American Council on Education; Associate of Science in Justice Administration, credit upon transfer from other institutions

5. **Credit for successful completion of standardized achievement tests:** Associate of Science in Home and Family Development, College-Level Examination Program (CLEP) General Examinations, College-Level Examination Program (CLEP) Subject Examinations, American College Testing (ACT) Proficiency Examination Program; Associate of Arts in Family and Local History Studies, none; Associate of Science in Justice Administration, College-Level Examination Program (CLEP) General Examinations, College-Level Examination Program (CLEP) Subject Examinations, College Board Advanced Placement Examinations, American College Testing (ACT) Proficiency Examination Program

6. **Number of credit hours required for degree:** Associate of Science in Home and Family Development and Associate of Arts in Family and Local History Studies, 64 semester hours; Associate of Science in Justice Administration, 67 semester hours

7. **Minimum campus time:** Associate of Science in Home and Family Development and Associate of Arts in Family and Local History Studies, none; Associate of Science in Justice Administration, a one- to three-day seminar on campus is required (1 semester hour)

8. **Instructional methods provided for off-campus learning:** Associate of Science in Home and Family Development, correspondence courses, packaged course and study guides; Associate of Arts in Family and Local History Studies, correspondence courses; Associate of Science in Justice Administration, correspondence courses, packaged course and study guides, sponsored experiential learning

9. **Student support services provided:** Associate of Science in Home and Family Development, academic advising; Associate of Arts in Family and Local History Studies, academic advising, financial aid, (limited), orientation, (written), career counseling, (limited); Associate of Science in Justice Administration, academic advising, orientation, counseling and testing, career counseling

10. **Available informational materials:** Associate of Science in Home and Family Development and Associate of Arts in Family and Local History Studies, student handbook of pertinent policies and procedures, program catalog, program brochure; Associate of Science in Justice Administration, program catalog, program brochure

11. **Grading system:** A, B, C, D, F, or other variation of scale using A, B, C

12. **Enrollment:** Associate of Science in Home and Family Development, 210; Associate of Arts in Family and Local History Studies, 217; Associate of Science in Justice Administration, 56

13. **Degrees conferred:** Associate of Science in Home and Family Development, 5 (estimated); Associate of Arts in Family and Local History Studies, 2; Associate of Science in Justice Administration, 3

14. **Year begun:** Associate of Science in Home and Family Development, 1976; Associate of Arts in Family and Local History Studies, 1977; Associate of Science in Justice Administration, 1971

15. **Out-of-state students:** Accepted; tuition same as for in-state students

VERMONT

Community College of Vermont

Box 81
Montpelier, VT 05602

1. **Degrees and areas of study:** Associate Degree in individually designed studies
2. **Institutional accreditation:** New England Association of Schools and Colleges
3. **Previous education required:** High school diploma or GED equivalent; this requirement may be waived if student passes a battery of basic skills tests
4. **Credit for prior learning:** Satisfactory completion of instruction offered by businesses, government agencies, labor unions, or professional or voluntary associations, and evaluated by the American Council on Education; credit upon transfer from other institutions; demonstrated experiential learning (life and occupational experiences); military educational experiences evaluated by the American Council on Education
5. **Credit for successful completion of standardized achievement tests:** College-Level Examination Program (CLEP) General Examinations, College-Level Examination Program (CLEP) Subject Examinations, DANTES Subject Standardized Tests (DSST)
6. **Number of credit hours required for degree:** 60 semester hours
7. **Minimum campus time:** None
8. **Instructional methods provided for off-campus learning:** Television courses, computer-assisted, self-paced instruction, packaged course and study guides, cooperative education, supervised field work; sponsored experiential learning, learning contracts based on independent study and small-group seminar programs
9. **Student support services provided:** Academic advising, financial aid, orientation, counseling and testing, career counseling
10. **Available informational materials:** Student handbook of pertinent policies and procedures, program brochure
11. **Grading system:** Primarily criterion-referenced; however, grades S—satisfactory completion/N—not satisfactory, or I—incomplete are also used for some courses
12. **Enrollment:** 750
13. **Degrees conferred:** over 600 (estimated)
14. **Year begun:** 1973
15. **Out-of-state students:** Accepted; tuition higher than for in-state students

Johnson State College

External Degree Program
Johnson, VT 05656

1. **Degrees and areas of study:** Bachelor of Arts or Bachelor of Science in individualized studies

2. **Institutional accreditation:** New England Association of Schools and Colleges

3. **Previous education required:** 60 semester hours

4. **Credit for prior learning:** Credit upon transfer from other institutions; military educational experiences evaluated by the American Council on Education

5. **Credit for successful completion of standardized achievement tests:** College-Level Examination Program (CLEP) General Examinations, College-Level Examination Program (CLEP) Subject Examinations, American College Testing (ACT) Proficiency Examination Program, DANTES Subject Standardized Tests (DSST)

6. **Number of credit hours required for degree:** 122 semester hours

7. **Minimum campus time:** None

8. **Instructional methods provided for off-campus learning:** Correspondence courses, television courses, guided instruction via telephone and mail, cooperative education, supervised field work; sponsored experiential learning

9. **Student support services provided:** Academic advising, financial aid, orientation, counseling and testing

10. **Available informational materials:** Student handbook of pertinent policies and procedures, program catalog, program brochure

11. **Grading system:** There is no predominant grading system; type of evaluation varies according to agreement between student and advisor/mentor/instructor

12. **Enrollment:** 150

13. **Degrees conferred:** 85

14. **Year begun:** 1977

15. **Out-of-state students:** Accepted; tuition higher than for in-state students

Vermont College of Norwich University

Department of Alternative Education
Northfield, VT 05602

Goddard Graduate Program of Vermont College
Montpelier, VT 05602

1. **Degrees and areas of study:** Bachelor of Arts (Liberal Arts with student-designed major)—Goddard Experimental Program in Further Education (GEPFE), Bachelor of Arts (Liberal Arts with student-designed major)—Goddard Adult Degree Program (ADP), Master of Arts (student-designed major), Master of Fine Arts in Writing

2. **Institutional accreditation:** New England Association of Schools and Colleges

3. **Previous education required:** Bachelor's, high school diploma or GED equivalent; Master's, Bachelor's degree

4. **Credit for prior learning:** GEPFE and ADP, satisfactory completion of instruction offered by businesses, government agencies, labor unions, or professional or voluntary associations, and evaluated by the American Council on Education; credit upon transfer from other institutions; demonstrated experiential learning (life and occupational experiences); military educational experiences evaluated by the American Council on Education

5. **Credit for successful completion of standardized achievement tests:** GEPFE and ADP, College-Level Examination Program (CLEP) Subject Examinations, College-Level Examination Program (CLEP) General Examinations, American College Testing (ACT) Proficiency Examination Program, DANTES Subject Standardized Tests (DSST), College Board Advanced Placement Examinations

6. **Number of credit hours required for degree:** Bachelor's, 120 semester hours; Master's, 30 semester hours; Master of Fine Arts, 48 semester hours

7. **Minimum campus time:** GEPFE, eight weekends per six-month semester (one weekend is Friday evening to Sunday noon). On-campus involvement includes seminars, study planning and evaluations; ADP, twelve consecutive days every six months for planning of independent-study project and evaluation; Master of Arts, none; Master of Fine Arts, twelve consecutive days every six months for planning of independent-study project, evaluation, poetry and short-fiction reading, and listening to readings by fellow students and visiting writers

8. **Instructional methods provided for off-campus learning:** GEPFE, guided instruction via telephone and mail, sponsored experiential learning; ADP, guided instruction via telephone and mail; Master of Arts, guided instruction via telephone and mail, cooperative education, supervised field work, sponsored experiential learning; Master of Fine Arts in Creative Writing, guided instruction via telephone and mail

9. **Student support services provided:** Academic advising, financial aid, orientation, counseling and testing, career counseling, job placement assistance

10. **Available informational materials:** GEPFE, ADP and Master of Arts, student handbook of pertinent policies and procedures and program catalog; Master of Fine Arts, student handbook of pertinent policies and procedures and program brochure

11. **Grading system:** GEPFE and ADP, credit/no credit, and each semester project (15 semester hours) is concluded with a thorough evaluation by the student and by the faculty advisor; these evaluations become part of the transcript record; Master of Arts and Master of Fine Arts, written narrative and faculty evaluations

12. **Enrollment:** GEPFE, 155; ADP, 130; Master of Arts, 195; Master of Fine Arts, 48

13. **Degrees conferred:** GEPFE, 60 since the program was transferred to Norwich University in June 1981; ADP, 100 since the program was transferred in June 1981; Master of Arts, 100 since the program was transferred in June 1981; Master of Fine Arts, 10 since the program was transferred in June 1981

14. **Year begun:** GEPFE, 1967 at Goddard College and transferred to Norwich University in 1981; ADP, 1963 at Goddard College and transferred to Norwich University in 1981; Master of Arts, 1970 at Goddard College and transferred to Norwich University in 1981; Master of Fine Arts, 1981

15. **Out-of-state students:** Accepted; tuition same as for in-state students

George Mason University

4400 University Drive
Fairfax, VA 22030

1. **Degrees and areas of study:** Bachelor of Individualized Study Degree
2. **Institutional accreditation:** Southern Association of Colleges and Schools
3. **Previous education required:** One to two years of college
4. **Credit for prior learning:** Satisfactory completion of instruction offered by businesses, government agencies, labor unions, or professional or voluntary associations, and evaluated by the American Council on Education; credit upon transfer from other institutions; demonstrated experiential learning (life and occupational experiences); military educational experiences evaluated by the American Council on Education
5. **Credit for successful completion of standardized achievement tests:** College-Level Examination Program (CLEP) General Examinations, (CLPE General Examinations earn one-half of the amount of credit recommended by CLEP only if student scores in 80th percentile or higher), College-Level Examination Program (CLEP) Subject Examinations, DANTES Subject Standardized Tests (DSST)
6. **Number of credit hours required for degree:** 120 semester hours, 30 of which must be completed in the Northern Virginia Consortium (Members of the Consortium are George Mason University [the host institution], Marymount College of Virginia, Northern Virginia Community College, the Falls Church Regional Center of the University of Virginia, and Virginia Polytechnic Institute and State University)
7. **Minimum campus time:** None
8. **Instructional methods provided for off-campus learning:** Video cassettes, television courses, cooperative education, supervised field work
9. **Student support services provided:** Academic advising, financial aid, orientation, counseling and testing, job placement assistance, career counseling
10. **Available informational materials:** Student handbook of pertinent policies and procedures, program catalog, program brochure, program newsletter
11. **Grading system:** A, B, C, D, F, or other variation of scale using A, B, C
12. **Enrollment:** 415
13. **Degrees conferred:** 383
14. **Year begun:** 1976
15. **Out-of-state students:** Accepted; tuition higher than for in-state students

Fairmont State College

Locust Avenue
Fairmont, WV 26554
Member of the West Virginia Board of Regents Bachelor of Arts Degree Program

1. **Degrees and areas of study:** Bachelor of Arts in individually designed studies
2. **Institutional accreditation:** North Central Association of Colleges and Schools
3. **Previous education required:** High school diploma or GED equivalent
4. **Credit for prior learning:** Satisfactory completion of instruction offered by businesses, government agencies, labor unions, or professional or voluntary associations, and evaluated by the American Council on Education; credit upon transfer from other institutions; demonstrated experiential learning (life and occupational experiences); military educational experiences evaluated by the American Council on Education
5. **Credit for successful completion of standardized achievement tests:** College-Level Examination Program (CLEP) General Examinations, College-Level Examination Program (CLEP) Subject Examinations
6. **Number of credit hours required for degree:** 128 semester hours
7. **Minimum campus time:** 15 semester hours earned at any one or combination of Board of Regents institutions
8. **Instructional methods provided for off-campus learning:** Correspondence courses, television courses, newspaper courses, guided instruction via telephone and mail, packaged course and study guides
9. **Student support services provided:** Academic advising, financial aid, orientation, counseling and testing, career counseling, job placement assistance
10. **Available informational materials:** Student handbook of pertinent policies and procedures, program brochure, portfolio preparation brochure
11. **Grading system:** A, B, C, D, F, or other variation of scale using A, B, C; and credit for experiential learning, CLEP, etc.
12. **Enrollment:** 400
13. **Degrees conferred:** 201
14. **Year begun:** 1975
15. **Out-of-state students:** Accepted; tuition higher than for in-state students only if courses are taken on campus

West Liberty State College

Regents Bachelor of Arts Degree Program
West Liberty, WV 26074
Member of the West Virginia Board of Regents Bachelor of Arts Degree Program

1. **Degrees and areas of study:** Bachelor of Arts

2. **Institutional accreditation:** North Central Association of Colleges and Schools

3. **Previous education required:** High school diploma or GED equivalent

4. **Credit for prior learning:** Satisfactory completion of instruction offered by businesses, government agencies, labor unions, or professional or voluntary associations, and evaluated by the American Council on Education; credit upon transfer from other institutions; demonstrated experiential learning (life and occupational experiences); military educational experiences evaluated by the American Council on Education

5. **Credit for successful completion of standardized achievement tests:** College-Level Examination Program (CLEP) General Examinations, College-Level Examination Program (CLEP) Subject Examinations, College Board Advanced Placement Examinations, American College Testing (ACT) Proficiency Examination Program, DANTES Subject Standardized Tests (DSST)

6. **Number of credit hours required for degree:** 128 semester hours

7. **Minimum campus time:** 15 semester hours

8. **Instructional methods provided for off-campus learning:** Television courses, newspaper courses, sponsored experiential learning

9. **Student support services provided:** Academic advising, financial aid, orientation, counseling and testing, career counseling, job placement assistance

10. **Available informational materials:** Student handbook of pertinent policies and procedures, program brochure

11. **Grading system:** A, B, C, D, F, or other variation of scale using A, B, C

12. **Enrollment:** 250

13. **Degrees conferred:** 200

14. **Year begun:** 1975

15. **Out-of-state students:** Accepted; tuition higher than for in-state students

University of Wisconsin-Green Bay

Extended Degree and Individualized Learning Programs
Green Bay, WI 54302

1. **Degrees and areas of study:** Bachelor of Arts, Bachelor of Science (individually designed studies), Bachelor of Arts in General Studies
2. **Institutional accreditation:** North Central Association of Colleges and Schools
3. **Previous education required:** Bachelor of Arts and Bachelor of Science, 1–2 years of college; Bachelor of Arts in General Studies, high school diploma or GED equivalent
4. **Credit for prior learning:** Satisfactory completion of instruction offered by businesses, government agencies, labor unions, or professional or voluntary associations, and evaluated by the American Council on Education; credit upon transfer from other institutions; demonstrated experiential learning (life and occupational experiences); military educational experiences evaluated by the American Council on Education
5. **Credit for successful completion of standardized achievement tests:** College-Level Examination Program (CLEP) General Examinations, College-Level Examination Program (CLEP) Subject Examinations, College Board Advanced Placement Examinations, American College Testing (ACT) Proficiency Examination Program, DANTES Subject Standardized Tests
6. **Number of credit hours required for degree:** 124 semester hours
7. **Minimum campus time:** Bachelor of Arts and Bachelor of Science, two meetings with professor per course-about two days each semester; Bachelor of Arts in General Studies, Adult Learning Seminar-one weekend
8. **Instructional methods provided for off-campus learning:** Bachelor of Arts and Bachelor of Science, guided instruction via telephone and mail, supervised field work, sponsored experiential learning; Bachelor of Arts in General Studies, correspondence courses, video cassettes, television courses, newspaper courses, guided instruction via telephone and mail, packaged course and study guides, sponsored experiential learning
9. **Student support services provided:** Academic advising, financial aid, orientation, counseling and testing, career counseling, job placement assistance
10. **Available informational materials:** Student handbook of pertinent policies and procedures, program catalog, program brochure
11. **Grading system:** A, B, C, D, F, or other variation of scale using A, B, C, and pass/fail, credit/no credit, or other variation of this scale
12. **Enrollment:** Bachelor of Arts and Bachelor of Science, 25; Bachelor of Arts in General Studies, 286

13. **Degrees conferred:** Bachelor of Arts and Bachelor of Science, 80 (estimated); Bachelor of Arts in General Studies, 20 (estimated)

14. **Year begun:** Bachelor of Arts and Bachelor of Science, 1971; Bachelor of Arts in General Studies, 1978

15. **Out-of-state students:** Bachelor of Arts and Bachelor of Science, accepted (tuition higher than for in-state students); Bachelor of Arts in General Studies, not accepted

University of Wisconsin—Parkside

Access Program
Box 2000
Kenosha, WI 53141

1. **Degrees and areas of study:** Bachelor of Arts in Culture of the Industrial Society

2. **Institutional accreditation:** North Central Association of Colleges and Schools

3. **Previous education required:** Two years of college

4. **Credit for prior learning:** Satisfactory completion of instruction offered by businesses, government agencies, labor unions, or professional or voluntary associations, and evaluated by the American Council on Education; credit upon transfer from other institutions; military educational experiences evaluated by the American Council on Education

5. **Credit for successful completion of standardized achievement tests:** College-Level Examination Program (CLEP) General Examinations, College-Level Examination Program (CLEP) Subject Examinations, American College Testing (ACT) Proficiency Examination Program, College Board Advanced Placement Examinations, DANTES Subject Standardized Tests (DSST)

6. **Number of credit hours required for degree:** 60 semester hours

7. **Minimum campus time:** Weekend course seminar at beginning of academic year; one or two field trips and meetings each semester

8. **Instructional methods provided for off-campus learning:** Guided instruction via telephone and mail, packaged course and study guides, supervised field work

9. **Student support services provided:** Academic advising, financial aid, orientation, counseling and testing, career counseling, job placement assistance

10. **Available informational materials:** Student handbook of pertinent policies and procedures, program brochure

11. **Grading system:** A, B, C, D, F, or other variation of scale using A, B, C

12. **Enrollment:** 24

13. **Degrees conferred:** None

14. **Year begun:** 1981

15. **Out-of-state students:** Not accepted

University of Wisconsin—Platteville

Extended Degree Program
510 Pioneer Tower
725 West Main Street
Platteville, WI 53818

1. **Degrees and areas of study:** Bachelor of Science in Business Administration
2. **Institutional accreditation:** North Central Association of Colleges and Schools
3. **Previous education required:** One year or less of college
4. **Credit for prior learning:** Satisfactory completion of instruction offered by businesses, government agencies, labor unions, or professional or voluntary associations, and evaluated by the American Council on Education; credit upon transfer from other institutions; demonstrated experiential learning (life and occupational experiences); military educational experiences evaluated by the American Council on Education
5. **Credit for successful completion of standardized achievement tests:** College-Level Examination Program (CLEP) Subject Examinations
6. **Number of credit hours required for degree:** 128 semester hours
7. **Minimum campus time:** None
8. **Instructional methods provided for off-campus learning:** Correspondence courses, television courses, guided instruction via telephone and mail, packaged course and study guides, cooperative education, supervised field work, sponsored experiential learning
9. **Student support services provided:** Academic advising, orientation, counseling, job placement assistance
10. **Available informational materials:** Program catalog, program brochure
11. **Grading system:** A, B, C, D, F, or other variation of scale using A, B, C
12. **Enrollment:** 450
13. **Degrees conferred:** 15
14. **Year begun:** 1978
15. **Out-of-state students:** Not accepted

University of Wisconsin—River Falls

College of Agriculture
River Falls, WI 54022

1. **Degrees and areas of study:** Bachelor of Science in Agriculture
2. **Institutional accreditation:** North Central Association of Colleges and Schools
3. **Previous education required:** High school diploma or GED equivalent
4. **Credit for prior learning:** Satisfactory completion of instruction offered by businesses, government agencies, labor unions, or professional or voluntary

associations, and evaluated by the American Council on Education; credit upon transfer from other institutions; demonstrated experiential learning (life and occupational experiences); military educational experiences evaluated by the American Council on Education

5. **Credit for successful completion of standardized achievement tests:** College-Level Examination Program (CLEP) General Examinations, College-Level Examination Program (CLEP) Subject Examinations, American College Testing (ACT) Proficiency Examination Program, College Board Advanced Placement Examinations, DANTES Subject Standardized Tests (DSST)

6. **Number of credit hours required for degree:** 192 quarter hours

7. **Minimum campus time:** None, although some time on campus for orientation is strongly encouraged and, depending on courses selected, some time on campus may be required for laboratory activities

8. **Instructional methods provided for off-campus learning:** Correspondence courses, video cassettes, television courses, newspaper courses, guided instruction via telephone and mail, computer-assisted, self-paced instruction, packaged course and study guides, cooperative education, supervised field work, sponsored experiential learning

9. **Student support services provided:** Academic advising, financial aid, orientation, counseling and testing, career counseling, job placement assistance

10. **Available informational materials:** Student handbook of pertinent policies and procedures, program catalog, program brochure

11. **Grading system:** A, B, C, D, F, or other variation of scale using A, B, C

12. **Enrollment:** 75

13. **Degrees conferred:** 2

14. **Year begun:** 1979

15. **Out-of-state students:** Not accepted, except for students from Minnesota because of the Wisconsin-Minnesota reciprocity agreement

University of Wisconsin—Superior

Extended Degree Program
Center for Continuing Education
1800 Grand Avenue
Superior, WI 54880

1. **Degrees and areas of study:** Bachelor of Arts or Bachelor of Science Degree in individually designed majors

2. **Institutional accreditation:** North Central Association of Colleges and Schools

3. **Previous education required:** One year or less of college

4. **Credit for prior learning:** Satisfactory completion of instruction offered by businesses, government agencies, labor unions, or professional or voluntary associations, and evaluated by the American Council on Education; credit upon transfer from other institutions; demonstrated experiential learning (life and

occupational experiences); military educational experiences evaluated by the American Council on Education

5. **Credit for successful completion of standardized achievement tests:** College-Level Examination Program (CLEP) General Examinations, College-Level Examination Program (CLEP) Subject Examinations, American College Testing (ACT) Proficiency Examination Program, College Board Advanced Placement Examinations

6. **Number of credit hours required for degree:** 192 quarter hours

7. **Minimum campus time:** Each course requires a minimum of two meetings with the instructor, scheduled at the student's convenience

8. **Instructional methods provided for off-campus learning:** Correspondence courses, video cassettes, television courses, newspaper courses, guided instruction via telephone and mail, packaged course and study guides, sponsored experiential learning

9. **Student support services provided:** Academic advising, financial aid, orientation, counseling and testing, career counseling, job placement assistance

10. **Available informational materials:** Student handbook of pertinent policies and procedures, program brochure, information packet for prospective students

11. **Grading system:** A, B, C, D, F, or other variation of scale using A, B, C

12. **Enrollment:** 450

13. **Degrees conferred:** 30

14. **Year begun:** 1978

15. **Out-of-state students:** Accepted; tuition higher for out-of-state students except for Minnesota residents who pay in-state fees

University of Wyoming

Laramie, WY 82071

1. **Degrees and areas of study:** Bachelor of Art or Bachelor of Science in Administration of Justice; Bachelor of Art or Bachelor of Science in Humanities/Fine Arts (B.A.) only, Social Sciences, and Natural Sciences/Mathematics; Bachelor of Social Work; Bachelor of Science in General Business Management; Bachelor of Science in Nursing; Bachelor of Art in Elementary Education

2. **Institutional accreditation:** North Central Association of Colleges and Schools

3. **Previous education required:** 65 semester hours of transferable college credit

4. **Credit for prior learning:** Credit upon transfer from other institutions

5. **Credit for successful completion of standardized achievement tests:** College-Level Examination Program (CLEP) Subject Examinations, College Board Advanced Placement Examinations

6. **Number of credit hours required for degree:** Bachelor of Art or Bachelor of Science in Administration of Justice and Bachelor of Art or Bachelor of Science in Humanities/Fine Arts, Social Sciences, and Natural Sciences/Mathematics, 120 semester hours; Bachelor of Social Work and Bachelor of Science in General Business Management, 128 semester hours; Bachelor of Science in Nursing and Bachelor of Art in Elementary Education, 130 semester hours

7. **Minimum campus time:** None

8. **Instructional methods provided for off-campus learning:** Bachelor of Art or Bachelor of Science in Administration of Justice, correspondence courses, television courses, cooperative education, sponsored experiential learning; Bachelor of Art or Bachelor of Science in Humanities/Fine Arts, Social Sciences, and Natural Sciences/Mathematics, correspondence courses, video cassettes, guided instruction via telephone and mail, cooperative education; Bachelor of Social Work, correspondence courses, guided instruction via telephone and mail, cooperative education, supervised field work; Bachelor of Science in General Business Management, correspondence courses, cooperative education, sponsored experiential learning; Bachelor of Science in Nursing, correspondence courses, video cassettes, packaged course and study guides, cooperative education, supervised field work; Bachelor of Art in Elementary Education, correspondence courses, guided instruction via telephone and mail, cooperative education, supervised field work, sponsored experiential learning

9. **Student support services provided:** Academic advising, financial aid, orientation, counseling and testing, job placement assistance, career counseling

10. **Available informational materials:** Program catalog, program brochure

11. **Grading system:** A, B, C, D, F, or other variation of scale using A, B, C

12. **Enrollment:** Bachelor of Art or Bachelor of Science in Administration of Justice,

6; Bachelor of Art or Bachelor of Science in Humanities/Fine Arts, Social Sciences, and Natural Sciences/Mathematics, 19; Bachelor of Social Work, 12; Bachelor of Science in General Business Management, 40; Bachelor of Science in Nursing, 69; Bachelor of Art in Elementary Education, 290

13. **Degrees conferred:** Bachelor of Art or Bachelor of Science in Administration of Justice, 4; Bachelor of Art or Bachelor of Science in Humanities/Fine Arts, Social Sciences, and Natural Sciences/Mathematics, 40; Bachelor of Social Work, 13; Bachelor of Science in General Business Management, 3; Bachelor of Science in Nursing, 13; Bachelor of Art in Elementary Education, 18

14. **Year begun:** Bachelor of Art or Bachelor of Science in Administration of Justice, 1981; Bachelor of Art or Bachelor of Science in Humanities/Fine Arts, Social Sciences, and Natural Sciences/Mathematics, 1976; Bachelor of Social Work, 1978; Bachelor of Science in General Business Management, 1980; Bachelor of Science in Nursing, 1978; Bachelor of Art in Elementary Education, 1981

15. **Out-of-state students:** Not accepted

Joint Statement on Transfer and Award of Academic Credit

This statement was developed by the three national associations whose member institutions are directly involved in the transfer and award of academic credit: the American Association of Collegiate Registrars and Admissions Officers, the American Council on Education, and the Council on Postsecondary Accreditation. The need for such a statement came from an awareness of the growing complexity of transfer policies and practices, which have been brought about, in part, by the changing contours of postsecondary education. With increasing frequency, students are pursuing their education in a variety of institutional and extrainstitutional settings. Social equity and the intelligent use of resources require that validated learning be recognized wherever it takes place.

The statement is intended to serve as a guide for instructions that are developing or reviewing policies dealing with transfer and award of credit. The statement is under periodic review by the three associations, and reactions to it would, of course, be welcome. Comments may be directed to Henry Spille, Director of the Office on Educational Credit and Credentials, ACE.

> J. W. Peltason, President
> American Council on Education

This statement is directed to institutions of postsecondary education and others concerned with the transfer of academic credit among institutions and award of academic credit for extrainstitutional learning. Basic to this statement is the principle that each institution is responsible for determining its own policies and practices with regard to the transfer and award of credit. Institutions are encouraged to review their policies and practices periodically to assure that they accomplish the institutions' objectives and that they function in a manner that is fair and equitable to students. Any statements, this one or others referred to, should be used as guides, not as substitutes, for institutional policies and practices.

Transfer of credit is a concept that now involves transfer between dissimilar institutions and curricula and recognition of extrainstitutional learning, as well as transfer between institutions and curricula with similar characteristics. As their personal circumstances and educational objectives change, students seek to have their learning, wherever and however attained, recognized by institutions where they enroll for further study. It is important for reasons of social equity and educational effectiveness, as well as the wise use of resources, for all institutions to develop reasonable and definitive policies and procedures for acceptance of transfer credit. Such policies and procedures should provide maximum consideration for the individual student who has changed institutions or objectives. It is the receiving institutions' responsibility to provide reasonable and definitive policies and procedures for determining a student's knowledge in required subject areas. All institutions have a responsibility to furnish transcripts and other documents necessary for a receiving institution to judge the quality and quantity of students' work. Institutions also have a responsibility to advise the students that the work *reflected* on the transcript *may or may not* be accepted by a receiving institution.

Interinstitutional Transfer of Credit

Transfer of credit from one institution to another involves at least three considerations:

(1) the educational quality of the institution from which the student transfers
(2) the comparability of the nature, content, and level of credit earned to that offered by the receiving institution
(3) the appropriateness and applicability of the credit earned to the programs offered by the receiving institution, in light of the student's educational goals.

Accredited Institutions

Accreditation speaks primarily to the first of these considerations, serving as the basic indicator that an institution meets certain minimum standards. Users of accreditation are urged to give careful attention to the accreditation conferred by accrediting bodies recognized by the Council on Postsecondary Accreditation (COPA). COPA has a formal process of recognition which requires that all accrediting bodies so recognized must meet the same standards. Under these standards, COPA has recognized a number of accrediting bodies, including

(1) regional accrediting commissions (which historically accredited the more traditional colleges and universities but which now accredit proprietary, vocational-technical, and single-purpose institutions as well)
(2) national accrediting bodies that accredit various kinds of specialized institutions
(3) certain professional organizations that accredit free-standing professional schools, in addition to programs within multipurpose institutions (COPA annually publishes a list of recognized accrediting bodies, as well as a directory of institutions accredited by these organizations).

Although accrediting agencies vary in the ways they are organized and in their statements of scope and mission, all accrediting bodies that meet COPA's standards of recognition function to assure that the institutions or programs they accredit have met generally accepted minimum standards for accreditation.

Comparability and Applicability

Comparability of the nature, content, and level of transfer credit and the appropriateness and applicability of the credit earned to programs offered by the receiving institution are as important in the evaluation process as the accreditation status of the institution at which the transfer credit was awarded. Since accreditation does not address these questions, this information must be obtained from catalogues and other materials and from direct contact between knowledgeable and experienced faculty and staff at both the receiving and sending institutions. When such considerations as comparability and appropriateness of credit are satisfied, however, the receiving institution should have reasonable confidence that students from accredited institutions are qualified to undertake the receiving institution's educational programs.

Admissions and Degree Purposes

At some institutions there may be differences between the acceptance of credit for admission purposes and the applicability of credit for degree purposes and the applicability of credit for degree purposes. A receiving institution may accept previous work, place a credit value on it, and enter it on the transcript. However, the previous work, because of its nature and not its inherent quality, may be determined to have no applicability to a specific degree to be pursued by the student.

Institutions have a responsibility to make this distinction, and its implications, clear to students before they decide to enroll. This should be a matter of full disclosure, with the best interests of the student in mind. Institutions also should make every reasonable effort to reduce the gap between credits accepted and credits applied toward an educational credential.

Unaccredited Institutions

Institutions of postsecondary education that are not accredited by COPA-recognized accrediting bodies may lack that status for reasons unrelated to questions of quality. Such institutions, however, cannot provide a reliable, third-party assurance that they meet or exceed minimum standards. That being the case, students transferring from such institutions may encounter special problems in gaining acceptance and transferring credits to accredited institutions. Institutions admitting students from unaccredited institutions should take special steps to validate credits previously earned.

Foreign Institutions

In most cases, foreign institutions are chartered and authorized by their national governments, usually through a ministry of education. Although this policy provides for a standardization within a country, it does not produce useful information about comparability from one country to another. No other nation has a system comparable to voluntary accreditation. The Division of Higher Education of the United Nations Educational, Scientific, and Cultural Organization (UNESCO) is engaged in a project to develop international compacts for the acceptance of educational credentials. At the operational level, four organizations—The Council on International Educational Exchange (CIEE), the National Council on the Evaluation of Foreign Student Credentials (CEC), the National Association for Foreign Student Admissions (NAFA), and the National Liaison Committee on Foreign Student Admissions (NLC)—often can assist institutions by distributing general guidelines on admission and placement of foreign students. Equivalency or placement recommendations are to be evaluated in terms of the programs and policies of the individual receiving institution.

Validation of Extrainstitutional and Experiential Learning for Transfer Purposes

Transfer-of-credit policies should encompass educational accomplishment attained in extrainstitutional settings as well as at accredited postsecondary institutions. In deciding on the award of credit for extrainstitutional learning, institutions will find the services of the American Council on Education's Office on Educational Credit and Credentials helpful. One of the Office's functions is to opereate and foster programs to determine credit equivalencies for various modes of extrainstitutional learning. The Office maintains evaluation programs for formally structured courses offered by the military, and civilian noncollegiate sponsors such as business, corporations, government agencies, and labor unions. Evaluation services are also available for examination programs, for occupations with validated job proficiency evaluation systems, and for correspondence courses offered by schools accredited by the National Home Study Council. The results are published in a Guide series. Another resource is the General Education Development (GED) Testing Program, which provides a means for assessing high school equivalency.

For learning that has not been validated through the ACE formal credit recommendations process or through credit-by-examination programs, institutions are urged to explore the Council for Advancement of Experiential learning (CAEL) procedures and processes.

Uses of this Statement

This statement has been endorsed by the three national associations most concerned with practices in the area of transfer and award of academic credit—the American Association of Collegiate Registrars and Admissions Officers, the American Council on Education, and the Council on Postsecondary Accreditation.

Institutions are encouraged to use this statement as a basis for discussions in developing or reviewing institutional policies with regard to transfer. If the statement reflects an institutions's policies, that institution might want to use this publication to inform faculty, staff, and students.

It is recommended that accrediting bodies reflect the essential precepts of this statement in their criteria.

Approved by the Executive Committee, American Association of Collegiate
  Registrars and Admissions Officers
  November 21, 1978

Approved by the American Council on Education/Commission on Educational
  Credit and Credentials
  December 5, 1978

Approved by the COPA Board
  October 10, 1978

Awarding Credit for Extrainstitutional Learning[1]

The following statement by the ACE Commission on Educational Credit and Credentials has been approved by the ACE Board of Directors and endorsed by the Council on Postsecondary Accreditation.

The American Council on Education recommends that postsecondary education institutions develop policies and procedures for measuring and awarding credit for learning attained outside their sponsorship.

American society abounds in resources for learning at the postsecondary level. Public, private, and proprietary education institutions exercise the central but not exclusive responsibility for instruction and learning. Associations, business, government, industry, the military, and unions sponsor formal instruction. In addition, independent study and reading, work experiences, the mass media, and social interaction contribute to learning and competency.

Full and effective use of all educational resources is a worthy educational and social goal. Achieving this goal will depend to a large extent on providing equitable recognition for extrainstitutional learning:

- Educational credentials have a significant bearing on the economic, professional, and social status of the individual. Thus, social equity requires that equivalent learning, regardless of where and how it is achieved, be incorporated into the system of records for learning and competency, and

[1]"Extrainstitutional learning" is defined as learning that is attained outside the sponsorship of legally authorized and accredited postsecondary education institutions. The term applies to learning acquired from work and life experiences, independent reading and study, the mass media, and participation in formal courses sponsored by associations, business, government, industry, the military, and unions.

- Recognition encourages learning and contributes to pedagogical effectiveness. Teaching students what they already know is both stultifying to them and wasteful of educational and personal resources.

Guidelines

1. Reliable and valid evaluation of student achievement is the sine qua non in awarding credit. Experience, whether acquired at work, in social settings, in the library, at home, or in the formal classroom, is in itself an inadequate basis for awarding credit. Increased attention in choosing evaluation procedures and techniques and more thorough evaluation are necessary when learning has been attained without participation in a program of study prescribed by an educational institution and offered by its faculty.

2. In determining whether it is appropriate to accept a student's extrainstitutional learning for credit, the governing considerations should be its applicability to the student's program of study, including graduation requirements, and the relationship of the learning to the institution's mission, curricula and standards for student achievement. Learning should be articulated, documented and measured in these terms.

3. Institutions should evaluate extrainstitutional learning only in subject-matter fields in which they have or can arrange for faculty expertise or where they can rely on nationally validated examinations or other procedures for establishing credit equivalences. Institutions should award credit in these areas only if the quality of learning meets their standards for student achievement. Normally, institutions should evaluate learning and award credit only in subject fields in which they offer courses or curricula. However, if the acquisition of college level learning outcomes has been demonstrated in an area not taught by the institution, but related to the student's program of study, an exception may and ought to be made.

4. Institutions awarding credit for extrainstitutional learning should develop clearly stated policies regarding administrative responsibility, student eligibility, means of assessment, recording of results on transcripts, storage of documentation, student fees, and maximum number of credits allowable. Information on these and related institutional policies and procedures should be disseminated to students and faculty for maximum awareness and utilization.

5. Institutional policy should include provision that the institution's policies and procedures for awarding credit for extrainstitutional learning should be subject to periodic reevaluation.

Supplemental References

Accredited Institutions of Postsecondary Education (1982–83). Edited by Sherry S. Harris. Washington, D.C.: ACE, 1982.

This is the definitive directory of postsecondary institutions in the United States. The 1982–83 volume reports on more than 4,500 postsecondary and specialized schools. The directory reports the memberships of the thirteen institutional accrediting commissions as well as specialized accreditation by thirty-five professional agencies in sixty-five fields. Candidates for accreditation are also reported. In addition, the directory notes major changes in two-year and four-year institutions, including openings and closings, mergers, name changes; the names and addresses of the chief executive officers of institutional and specialized accrediting agencies; and briefly describes the accrediting process. Fully indexed. ($17.50)

American Council on Education. *Guide to Credit by Examination.* Washington, D.C.: ACE, 1981.

This first edition of a much needed volume provides registrars, admission officers, counselors, librarians, and college administrators with a thorough overview of the major programs and tests available as well as the quality of each. It may also be helpful in locating examinations that can be used to assess extrainstitutional learning. Test reviews and recommendations for more than 150 tests are included. Each recommendation is based on reviews by teams of faculty experts. The *Guide* contains a complete description of the evaluation process. ($27)

———*Guide to the Evaluation of Educational Experiences in the Armed Services* (1982 ed.). Washington, D.C.: ACE, 1982.

This biennial publication is the standard reference work on awarding credit for military learning experiences. It is designed to assist in the academic advising of students and in the placing of persons in training programs and jobs. The *Guide* contains credit recommendations for formal courses offered by the Department of Defense and the branches of the armed services and for educational credit in Army enlisted military occupational specialities and Navy Ratings. ($38)

————*The National Guide to Educational Credit for Training Programs* (1982–83 ed.). Washington, D.C.: ACE, 1982.

This annual reference is designed to help postsecondary institutions make effective decisions about granting credit to students who have completed courses outside their sponsorship. The revised and greatly expanded 1982–83 edition reports credit recommendations for approximately 1,700 courses offered by 144 organizations nationwide, including businesses, industries, labor unions, government agencies, and professional and voluntary associations. The *National Guide* includes recommendations for a selection of apprentice programs and for correspondence courses accredited by the National Home Study Council. The recommendations are based on evaluations conducted by teams of faculty experts as part of the ACE's Program on Noncollegiate Sponsored Instruction. The *National Guide* contains a complete description of the evaluation process. ($27)

Forrest, Aubrey. *Assessing Prior Learning—A CAEL Student Guide.* Columbia, Md.: Council for the Advancement of Experiential Learning, 1977.

It is typically the adult student who petitions for college credit based on prior experiential learning, and this *Student Guide* is directed to that audience. The purpose is to assist such adults in maximizing the value of their prior learning in relation to educational goals and successfully obtaining appropriate credit. The reader is led step by step through the process of identifying learning outcomes, relating them to educational goals, documenting experience, measuring learning outcomes, and requesting credit or recognition. ($5)

Hayenga, Sharon; Adams, Laura; and Rowe, Norma. *How to Choose: A Consumer's Guide to Understanding Colleges.* Columbia, Md.: Council for the Advancement of Experiential Learning, 1981.

Today there are more options for adult students than ever before. This guide helps adults who are thinking about returning to school, or have decided to do so, to identify and evaluate their options. The aim of the guide is to help prepare adults to make a well-informed choice about which school to attend. It sets forth an overall description of the different types of schools students can choose from, where adults can get information about schools, an explanation of information found in college catalogs, special considerations adult students should bear in mind when comparing programs at different schools, tips about applying for admission, and a general overview of financial aid opportunities for adult students. ($5)

McIntyre, Valerie. *Wherever You Learned It: A Directory of Opportunities for Educational Credit.* Edited by Ruth Cargo. Columbia, Md.: Council for the Advancement of Experiential Learning, 1981.

This directory lists more than 500 colleges and universities where a student can ask for credit for learning acquired outside school. It is especially aimed at adults who are thinking about going to college or going back to college and who feel they deserve recognition for what they have learned through work or other experiences. The colleges and universities listed in the directory use individualized assessment to grant regular college credit for prior learning—colleve-level experiential learning comparable to learning that occurs in the college classroom. Adults and their counselors can use the directory to help select a school or schools to contact about credit for prior learning. The directory is a set of five regional volumes. ($10 per volume; $45 for the set of five)

National University Continuing Education Association. *The Independent Study Catalog: NUCEA's Guide to Independent Study through Correspondence Instruction* (1983–85). Princeton, N.J.: Peterson's Guide.

This catalog is an updated and expanded version, listing more than 12,000 correspondence study courses in over 1,000 subject-matter areas, plus such extensive explanatory information about correspondence study as admission and time requirements, accreditation, enrollment, registration forms and catalogues, exams, study assignments, transfer of credit, and financial considerations and financial aid. Courses are organized into four sections—high school, undergraduate, graduate, and noncredit courses—with separate indexes. Capsule profiles of each institution include contact person and address, availability of credit courses on a noncredit basis, policies on overseas enrollment, courses for gifted high school students, and unusual programs available. All but one of the 72 institutions of higher education listed are accredited.
Available from NUCEA Book Order Department, P. O. Box 2123, Princeton, New Jersey 08540. ($7.30)

CAEL. *You Deserve the Credit: A Guide to Receiving Credit for Non-College Learning*. Columbia, Md.: Council for the Advancement of Experiential Learning, 1981.

This guide is designed to help learners become familiar with the many options available to them as they seek recognition for their noncollege learning achievements. An understanding of how colleges determine credit can help the adult returning to school know what to expect, prepare for assessment, and select a school that offers the types of assessment opportunities he or she is seeking. ($5)

American Council on Education
The American Council on Education, founded in 1918 and composed of institutions of higher education and national and regional education associations, is the nation's major coordinating body for postsecondary education. Through voluntary and cooperative action, the council provides comprehensive leadership for improving educational standards, policies, procedures, and services.

Office on Educational Credit and Credentials
The Office on Educational Credit and Credentials is the council office concerned with credit and credentialing policies and practices in postsecondary education. The

role of the office and of its policy-making and advisory arm, the Commission on Educational Credit and Credentials, is to give attention to educational credit and credentialing policies for postsecondary education, to foster high standards and sound practices for the evaluation and recognition of extrainstitutional learning, to advise institutions for postsecondary education on how these credit equivalents can be used in placing students in academic programs and in credentialing educational accomplishment, to assist institutions for postsecondary education in officially recognizing an individual's competency, knowledge, and skills, wherever and however obtained, and to provide adults with an alternative means of demonstrating high school graduation competencies.

Index A: Institutions

Index B: Areas of Study

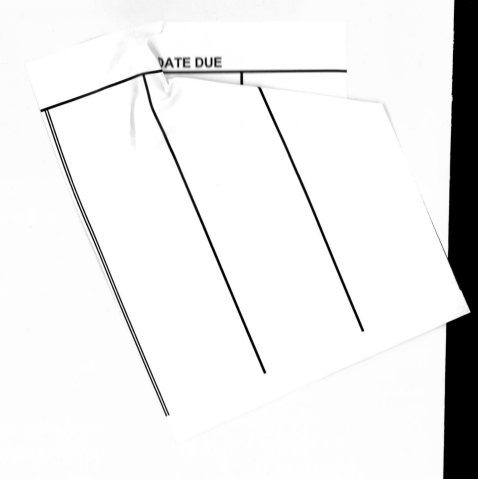

DATE DUE